The Politics of the Global

BORDERLINES

A BOOK SERIES CONCERNED WITH REVISIONING GLOBAL POLITICS
Edited by David Campbell and Michael J. Shapiro

For more books in the series, see p. vi.

The Politics of the Global

HIMADEEP MUPPIDI

BORDERLINES, VOLUME 23

 University of Minnesota Press

Minneapolis

London

Published by the University of Minnesota Press
111 Third Avenue South, Suite 290
Minneapolis, MN 55401-2520
http://www.upress.umn.edu

Library of Congress Cataloging-in-Publication Data

Muppidi, Himadeep.
    The politics of the global / Himadeep Muppidi.
        p. cm. — (Borderlines ; v. 23)
    Includes bibliographical references and index.
    ISBN 0-8166-4247-8 (hardcopy : alk. paper) — ISBN 0-8166-4248-6
(pbk. : alk. paper)
        1. Globalization. I. Title. II. Borderlines (Minneapolis, Minn.) ; v. 23.
    JZ1318.M865 2004
    327.1'7—dc22

                                                            2003025760

Printed in the United States of America on acid-free paper

The University of Minnesota is an equal-opportunity educator and employer.

12 11 10 09 08 07 06 05 04   10 9 8 7 6 5 4 3 2 1

For my parents
Rajini and Janardhan Muppidi

and in memory of my uncle
Krupakar Muppidi

BORDERLINES

Contents

Acknowledgments

Emerging as this book does from a number of conversations, I see its publication as the provisional fixing—the making public—of an ongoing and necessarily incomplete interpretive process. As with any dialogical endeavor, multiple and diverse others (people, texts, institutions) have played a crucial role in this process. So with considerable gratitude I wish to acknowledge their contributions while absolving them of responsibility for my idiosyncratic interpretations of these conversations.

My most general debt is to those scholars who have, in recent years, opened the discipline of international relations to various forms of critical inquiry. Their creative reworking of international relations has made it possible to see the discipline as something more than an ideology of the dominant powers.

I have benefited immensely from the intellectually rich, warmly communal, and deeply reflective environment nurtured by the Department of Political Science at the University of Minnesota. It was a wonderfully enriching experience to be in almost daily conversation with, among others, Tarak Barkawi, Shampa Biswas, Monali Chowdhurie, Andy Davison, Lei Guang, Mark Laffey, Jennifer Milliken, Sheila Nair, Darel Paul, Diana Saco, Benjamin Tolosa, and Jutta Weldes. My thanks to them for helping me think through many of the issues in this book.

Among a number of demanding teachers at the University of

Minnesota, Bud Duvall was most critical in shaping my thinking on the constitution of the global. The design of this particular project owes much to many long conversations with him. I am especially grateful to him for suggesting, at an early stage in the preparation of this manuscript, that I enlarge my focus on the global economy to include issues of global security and global governance. Exemplary scholar-adviser-mentor, Bud personifies the best qualities of intellectual life in academia.

At Vassar College, I have been fortunate to find both an academic and social home. The privilege of participating in an intellectually intense, highly supportive, deliberately and deliberatively democratic departmental culture has been further enhanced by the sustained friendship of Andy Davison and Katie Hite. The intellectual depth and rigor of my departmental colleagues as well as the idealistic temperament of the students have made teaching at Vassar a truly enjoyable and an existentially meaningful experience.

From the broader field of international relations, Sanjoy Bannerjee, Michael Barnett, David Blaney, Kurt Burch, Neta Crawford, Lisa Disch, Orfeo Fioretos, Naeem Inayatullah, Mark Laffey, Kathryn Sikkink, and Alexander Wendt have, at different stages of this project, offered helpful advice, insightful criticisms, and welcome suggestions for improving my arguments. I am indebted to them for their personal goodwill, intellectual generosity, and unstintingly critical gaze.

Mark Rupert and Timothy Sinclair reviewed the manuscript for the University of Minnesota Press and offered many excellent suggestions and advice. I suspect that, like many of my interlocutors, they probably disagree with my particular perspective on the politics of the global. But their criticisms and feedback helped make this book much stronger than it otherwise would have been. I have really enjoyed working with the University of Minnesota Press. I am deeply appreciative of Carrie Mullen's enthusiastic support for and excellent advice on many aspects of this project. Thanks are also due to Nancy Sauro for her meticulous copyediting of the manuscript.

I am grateful to some of the current students in the Department of Political Science, University of Minnesota, particularly Ayten Gundogdu, Jonathan Havercroft, Wanjiru Kamau, Helen Kinsella, Meghana Nayak, Amit Ron, Amy Skonieczny, Ann Towns, and Latha Varadarajan, for inviting me to present a chapter from this book at the Minnesota International Relations Colloquium and for their many useful comments and criticisms.

Meaningful concerns in intellectual inquiry rarely emerge from or stay confined within narrow academic or disciplinary boundaries. The politics of the global was never, from that perspective, a purely academic issue for me. Questions of colonialism, cosmopolitanism, modernity, and subalternity were also necessarily questions about the reproduction or transformation of particular selves and spaces within historical contexts. A number of friends, many of long-standing duration, have engaged me in frequently pleasurable, sometimes bitingly sharp, but always critical reflections on these questions. I acknowledge my debt to Jehangir Aziz, David Blaney, Christopher Chekuri, Andy Davison, Dharmendra Gaddam, Naeem Inayatullah, Prabhakara Jha, Sangeetha Kamat, Shashidhar Kaparthi, Sankaran Krishna, Rama Mantena, Biju Mathew, Kuo Pahai, Anila Prabhu, V. Rajagopal, Rajesh Rajagopalan, Velcheru Narayana Rao, Samarender Reddy, and Srinivas Surabhi. As profoundly thoughtful friends, incisive critics, and committed activists at various levels, they have been excellent role models in many ways.

One of the pleasures of traveling to India in recent years has been the intellectual and social companionship of Raji and Rajesh Rajagopalan, Satya and P. Narasimha, Kashyap and Udita Chandra, and Varun Sahni. My thanks to them for their enduring friendship and warm hospitality.

My immediate and extended family—territorially dispersed but emotionally woven together—has, as always, been an immense source of support and intellectual strength. I can do little but be grateful for that not always fully deserved privilege. To my parents, to whom this book is dedicated, I owe more than I can ever acknowledge. Their foresight and sacrifices have made everything possible for me.

The research for this book was supported in part by a junior fellowship from the American Institute of Indian Studies (Chicago), a special doctoral dissertation grant from the Graduate School of the University of Minnesota, and a travel grant from the Dean of Faculty Fund, Vassar College. I am deeply appreciative of the support offered by these institutions at crucial stages of the project.

Introduction
The Local and the Global

Naravarapally Chandrababu Naidu is the chief minister of Andhra Pradesh, a state in the southern part of India. The political party he heads, the Telugu Desam, is a regional party that came to power by espousing issues of local pride against national parties such as the Congress.[1] Even with a political base confined to Andhra Pradesh, Naidu has, since 1996, played an important role in sustaining different ruling coalitions at the level of the national government. Notwithstanding that role, Naidu has confined his politics to safeguarding the regional interests of Andhra Pradesh, turning down offers of national positions including, at one stage, the prime ministership of India.

But Naidu is also unusual in seeing himself not just as a regional politician but also as the CEO of A.P. (Andhra Pradesh) Inc. Adopting an explicitly managerial approach to governing the state, Naidu notes that a chief minister is a CEO in that "[he] is accountable to his stakeholders. He has vision, short-term and long-term. He uses technology to improve productivity and is professional in his approach."[2] For an Indian context, as one political observer pointed out, "[a] Chief Minister as CEO seems an oxymoron. The one connotes a *sarkari* [government] culture of bureaucratic delays and red tape; the other implies drive and risk-taking zeal."[3]

One could be excused then for thinking that Naidu's managerial approach to the state is but a new way of carving out a political niche in the cutthroat world of Indian politics. Naidu himself, in frequently changing his alliances, has given more than enough reason to support such a view.[4] But Naidu as CEO has articulated a specific set of interests for A.P. Inc. His public presentations dwell constantly on the poor position of India (in the bottom five) in the Global Competitiveness Reports of the World Economic Forum. Arguing that India needs to achieve a position of leadership in the twenty-first century, Naidu offers a concrete strategy—a Vision 2020 program—for A.P. Inc.[5]

While malleable on political ideology, Naidu is very explicit about his plans for A.P. Inc. He observes, "My vision is to make Andhra Pradesh the foremost state in India in ten years' time in terms of the standard of living of my people."[6] How does he propose to do that? According to Naidu, this can be done by increasing Andhra Pradesh's ability to be nationally and globally competitive, which implies treating domestic and international private investment as the "prime engine of growth," as well as integrating information technology into the different dimensions of development and governance.

Pursuing Andhra Pradesh's national and global competitiveness, Naidu has concentrated on restructuring two key areas: the state's economy and its government. He has launched a series of economic restructurings that have made Andhra Pradesh a favored destination of foreign investment in India. There are many indicators of the success of Naidu's efforts, but the most notable is the decision of Microsoft to locate its software development center not in Bangalore—a long-favored destination of foreign investment—but in Hyderabad.[7] His economic reforms have been praised by the World Bank and resulted in A.P. Inc. becoming the first state in India to enjoy direct lending from the World Bank.[8]

For the state government, Naidu argues for SMART ("simple, moral, accountable, responsive and transparent") governance.[9] As a signpost for what a government should be, he quotes an official report from Australia: "The public will expect government services to be comparable with the best services available from the private sector in terms of quality, accuracy, timeliness and user-friendliness. Clients will no longer tolerate delays, bureaucratic mistakes or excessively time-consuming and difficult procedures."[10]

Naidu sees this model of governance as achievable through the use of information technology (IT). IT, he believes, would facilitate the constant monitoring of the government's work by the CEO and a responsive public. He has thus been in the forefront of introducing information technology systems that would allow for the constant tracking of government files, the public monitoring of the performance of government programs, and the easy access of the public to government databases.

One editorial writer observed about Naidu: "Inspired by Federal Express's ability to pinpoint the location of any package anywhere in the world using information technology, despite handling more than two million packages a day, Naidu wants his bureaucrats to tell him why a government file cannot be similarly tracked using the same technology. He has drawn up elaborate plans to computerize every government activity from the mandal level to the departments in the state secretariat; he wants to get rid of the complex hierarchies, elaborate procedures, and slow decision making in government." Obviously impressed by Naidu's efforts, the editorial writer continues, "Mr. Naidu has understood that the basis of fast growth and development is good governance. Far more important than soliciting visits abroad, ruinous tax concessions and brilliant announcements is systemic change to make administration administer. Naidu disproves the notion that Indian politicians are sense-proof."[11]

While Naidu's focus on leadership and economic competitiveness, his managerial approach to governance, and his faith in information technology are fascinating, more remarkable are his efforts to ferret out employment opportunities—"window[s] of opportunity"—for his constituents abroad, particularly in the United States.[12] His job, it appears, is to globalize A.P. Inc. even as he tries to make it an attractive locale for various others.

Consider the ironies. Here is a politician who is primarily a local, not a national, actor. This politician is so local that he turns down national roles except insofar as they allow him the political space to take care of his provincial, subnational interests. But this very same local politician talks about the economy and the polity in an increasingly global language, using terms such as "competitiveness," "pro-activeness," and "core competencies" that tumble straight out of American management texts and gurus; proffers Singapore, Australia, Malaysia, and New Zealand as exemplars of what he wants to achieve in Andhra Pradesh; and, most surprising of all, pursues economic strategies that assume employment opportunities for his constituents in the United States and the rest of the world.[13] It needs to be remembered that Andhra Pradesh is not a sovereign actor in the international system, nor does it have any special treaties with the United States or the rest of the world.[14]

But consider another "local" event. On May 18, 1998, the U.S. Senate passed a bill that increased the number of "skilled foreigners" allowed into the territory of the United States every year.[15] This bill, called the American Competitiveness Bill, was passed to improve U.S. competitiveness in the international system and thereby promote American national interests.[16] While the domestic American reaction to this bill was nothing noteworthy, it was warmly received thousands of miles away in Andhra Pradesh's capital city of Hyderabad.[17] How does a local American event resonate abroad, thousands of miles away in a foreign space, but fail to do so domestically? Could one say that the Hyderabadis, though foreign in one sense, were already at home in the United States, more so than many American citizens?

THE GLOBALIZATION OF SECURITY

Addressing the UN General Assembly in 1997, U.S. President Bill Clinton "challenged [it] to build new institutions to make globalization work for all people" and announced that the United States would do its part to ensure "global security and prosperity into the 21st century." Pursuing these goals required, President Clinton argued, a Comprehensive Test Ban Treaty (CTBT), a permanent international court, and a "streamlined" UN. Expanding on their necessity, he asserted that a CTBT would "mark an historic milestone in our efforts to reduce the nuclear threat and build a safer world," a permanent international court was needed to "defend and extend universal human rights" and "prosecute the most serious violations of humanitarian law," and a "streamlined" UN would make it "more efficient and better able to serve the world community."[18]

Contrast this with the challenge posed by President Bush to the UN in September 2002. Challenging the UN to deal with issues of "global terror" and after appealing to and outlining various "standards of human dignity shared by all" and a "system of security defended by all," President Bush invested "one place" and "one regime"—Iraq—with "all these dangers."[19] Though global terror was territorialized, in this instance, to one province in the world, the Bush administration has not shown much sympathy for other forms of globality ranging from global warming accords to the International Criminal Court. Despite that, the very first paragraph of the National Security Strategy (NSS) issued by it portrays a world governed by global norms.[20]

According to the NSS, "The great struggles of the twentieth century between liberty and authoritarianism ended with a decisive victory for forces of freedom—and a single sustainable model for national success: freedom, democracy, and free enterprise." While rejecting the norms structuring the various global regimes (nuclear and environmental), the Bush administration posits values that are global in a different way. Now, it asserts, there is only a "single, sustainable model for national success." The "values of freedom" that it identifies are global in a way that the nuclear security regime probably was not: they are "right and true for every person, in every society," and the "duty of protecting these values" covers "people across the globe and across the ages." What we have then is not a regime that rejects *global* norms but a regime with a seemingly different understanding of what these norms are. Notwithstanding their disagreements, the Clinton and the Bush administrations both articulate their claims in the language of globality.

These events, concerning issues of the global economy and global security, raise some critical questions about the nature of the global in the contemporary world. What is the significance of a provincial politician in a developing country speaking the language of American corporate managers and structuring his local economy according to their needs? Why do American regulations about U.S. national competitiveness resonate abroad more than at home? How is it that U.S. policy makers assert global claims even as they go about deliberately and unilaterally ignoring existing global regimes and voices?

One way to read these events is to see them as expressive, in many ways, of the coming to prominence of various discourses of globalization. Central to such discourses are contestations over the social meanings of the global. It is the politics of production of this global that I want to explore. With that in view, I examine, in chapter 1, the dominant claims about globalization in conventional (rationalist, constructivist, and historical-materialist) international relations and show how many prominent theorists of international relations reproduce a colonial politics in their conceptualizations of globality. I offer, in chapter 2, a critical constructivist framework that helps overcome such limitations in analyzing the politics of globalization. I utilize this framework in chapters 3 and 4 to explain how the politics of globalization plays itself out on the historical and ideological terrain of two multicultural democracies. Chapter 5 examines the question of how various productions of the global take place across national borders despite critical differences in social meanings and historical identities. I demonstrate, in this chapter, the different political possibilities (e.g., colonial coercion, postcolonial ambivalence, and postcolonial co-option) that are opened by the global relays of meanings, identities, and power. The book concludes with a brief exploration of the spaces and strategies for resisting the colonization of the global.

1

Colonial Globalities

Here, at a crossroads five miles east of the Iraqi capital, Marines shot dead eight civilians and injured seven more, including a child who was shot in the face. All the civilians were traveling out of Baghdad on Friday night in vehicles which, the Marines say, refused to stop when challenged—in English—and, when warning shots were fired, accelerated. . . . Lance Corporal Eric Jewell said: "We didn't know what was in that bus. It may sound bad, but I'd rather see more of them dead than any of my friends. . . . Everyone understands the word 'stop,' right?"

JAMES MEEK, OBSERVER

One of the fascinating, but probably unintended, aspects of Adam Hochschild's powerful account of the Belgian colonization of the Congo is the bewilderment experienced by the educated Westerner on learning about mass killings under European colonialism. At the very beginning of the book, Hochschild recounts how he was startled to learn, in a footnote, about the five to eight million lives lost to slave labor in the Congo. Hochschild calculates correctly that, even with vastly reduced numbers, that footnote in history would easily make the Congo one of the "major killing grounds of modern times." "Why," he wonders, "were these deaths not mentioned in the *standard* litany of *our* century's horrors?" "And why," he asks, had *he* "never before heard of them?" Hochschild's agonized questioning of himself and the history he happened to have read as the "standard litany of our century" is interesting in itself. But what really intensifies that painful discovery of a lack is his acute sense of himself as someone who had been "writing about human rights for years" and who had traveled many times to Africa and even to the Congo (1998, 3).

As Hochschild tries to make sense of this lack of knowledge within the well-educated, well-traveled, humane self, it becomes clear, to the reader at least, that it was not knowledge that was lacking as much as the appropriate imaginary within which such knowledge would have made sense. Groping back in time, Hochschild recollects a conversation with a drunken CIA official boasting about the assassination of Patrice Lumumba and a text—Joseph Conrad's *Heart of Darkness*—that had already dealt with some of these things, but he recalls having "filed away" Conrad "under fiction, not fact" (3). Now, searching for "facts," Hochschild discovers a "vast river of words" (5)—memoirs, records, government reports, travel accounts, and journals by Westerners. But this "vast river of words," Hochschild recognizes, flows invisibly in the larger imaginary of Western history, for neither in the capitals nor in the museums of European colonial powers were there any monuments or signs for the millions who were murdered under colonialism.

This pattern of hearing a fragment of a story, of being startled by the commonsensical knowledge of mass killings under European colonialism, and then subsequently discovering proof of it in a "vast river of words" flowing around oneself is repeated with Jules Marchal, a former Belgian ambassador to Ghana, Liberia, and Sierra Leone in West Africa. Like Hochschild, Jules Marchal encounters a story of millions killed that he takes to be an obvious slander, takes a journey back into the archives to refute it, discovers its irrefutable truth, and is suddenly able to make sense of earlier conversations and fragments of talk he had heard in the Congo.

Marchal remembers, in particular, the year 1948 and a corporal in the Congo saying to him, "The rubber *this* time, that was nothing. But the first time, *that* was terrible" (Hochschild 1998, 299). The corporal was comparing the tapping of rubber during the Second World War relatively favorably with the one at the turn of the nineteenth century, but it takes Jules Marchal, the Belgian ambassador to West Africa, thirty years and a deliberate effort to educate himself out of his provinciality before he could understand what the corporal was saying about Belgium's history.

Compared with the systematic erasures of these histories in Europe, and reading against Hochschild's incorrect claim about the silence of Africans, the materiality of this knowledge in various parts of Africa is clear. It is therefore not surprising at all that Marchal's education begins when he decides to correct a "slander" in a Liberian newspaper that referred to the ten million killed in the Congo of King Leopold. Hochschild himself points out that "[i]n the Mongo tongue, 'to send someone to harvest rubber' is an idiom meaning 'to tyrannize'" (1998, 300). In other words, the knowledge of colonialism is monumentalized and materialized in various ways in Africa. It was not knowledge that was lacking, it was knowing how to read that knowledge, knowing how to go beyond the self in understanding the world. What was missing was, following Spivak (Landry and Maclean 1996, 295), "global literacy." It is from this perspective that the dominant narratives of international relations appear particularly provincial and relatively illiterate in their attempts to read the global.

THE PROVINCIALITY OF INTERNATIONAL RELATIONS

Prominent perspectives on globalization in international relations can be classified into three distinctive narratives: the rationalist, historical-materialist, and constructivist. Each narrative, undoubtedly, consists of many theories, some of them disagreeing strongly with each other. Notwithstanding their differences, each narrative is united through shared modes of understanding and explanation that seek to go beyond the international to access the global. In what follows I read these dominant traditions to show the limitations of their current attempts to reach beyond the international.

RATIONALISM

Rationalist-liberals understand the global primarily as "networks of interdependence" (Nye 2001). These "networks" are seen as having emerged or "thickened" recently (Keohane 2000). They are presented as promoting an interdependence that extends not just across the economic realm but also into "environmental, military, social and political" ones (Nye 2001). The primary effect of these "networks" is the "shrinkage of distance on a world scale" (Keohane 2000). Compared with liberals, rationalist-neorealists hold out for a broader conception of the global as going beyond "networks," to some form of "integration." As Waltz (1999) observes, "The difference between an interdependent and an integrated world is a qualitative one and not a mere matter of proportionality."

To their credit, both liberals and neorealists recognize some of the nuances involved in conceptualizing the global. Keohane gestures toward that complexity when he draws, however briefly, on Arjun Appadurai's (1996) concept of "diasporic public spheres"; Joseph Nye hints negatively at it when he notes the absence of a strong sense of political community at the global level; and Kenneth Waltz (1999), though arguing that current levels of interdependence have not yet matched those that existed at the beginning of the last century, admits that "one feels that the world has become a smaller one." This attempt to comprehend the global as a specific type of public space, a community, or even an intensified feeling is a positive move on the part of rationalists, indicating as it does a deeply felt need to go beyond the imaginative horizons of conventional international relations. Despite this desire, rationalists rarely move to explore the intersubjective and coconstituted nature of the global. Not surprisingly, the questions they ask of the global emerge primarily from the spaces of domestic politics and center on issues of global governance (Waltz 1999; Keohane 2000) and global democracy (Nye 2001). But rationalists are either unable or unwilling to explore how different understandings of the global might affect questions of governance and of democracy.

Both Kenneth Waltz and Robert Keohane turn to the globalization at the beginning of the twentieth century to argue that the high degree of interdependence in contemporary times is nothing new. But, keeping with their neglect of social meanings, they do not bother to inquire if that particular global was understood the same way across the world. Indicators of trade, capital flows, and labor mobility aside, a majority of the world's inhabitants were directly or indirectly under colonial rule during the putatively first phase of globalization. Globalization, for a majority of the world's people, was then directly constituted as colonialism (Davis 2001).

Is globalization as colonization an issue worth considering before one moves to the question of what lessons we can learn about governance of democracy? Probably not, since one of the lessons that Keohane seeks to draw out is what sort of institutions are needed to foster "effective" and "right" governance. Not surprisingly, none of these lessons emerges from a consideration of the experience of those who were forcibly globalized in that particular phase. Keohane's arguments about the "effective" dimension come from the work on institutions in political science and the "right" part comes from the normative theory of liberalism. Keohane, therefore, proposes a "liberalism of fear" to complement the conventional focus on the "liberalism of progress" but fails to grasp the deeper "fear of liberalism" and "fear of progress" that exist in the once-colonized world.

Nye (2001), on the other hand, tackles the critical question of a "democratic deficit" at the global level. Arguing that understandings of "we, the people" at the global level are relatively weak, he points to the undemocratic nature of according one state one vote given that such a move would give more power to the citizen of a small country (the Maldive Islands) than of a large one (such as China). Fair enough. But is Nye going to be truly radical here and consider the world itself as "a single global constituency"? Nye rules that out on the grounds that in such a global constituency the majority would prevail and this would mean that the "2 billion Chinese and Indians could usually get their way." He adds, for good measure, that this would be an unwelcome scenario for antiglobalization NGOs agitating for environmental and labor standards since these issues garner little sympathy from the officials of these two countries.

A number of things are problematic here. I will confine my attention to two. First, Nye's argument for the merits of democracy appear to be based not on its inherently positive traits but on the consequences that it is likely to generate for various national or group constituencies. Democracy, at the global level, is a procedural principle rather than a desirable normative principle. Second, he presumes a global in which national identity continues as the main organizing principle of politics. Indians and Chinese, he assumes, will vote as Indians and Chinese (i.e., according to their national rather than individual or global identities) and according to the preferences of their government officials. Why would Nye assume that a billion Indians and more than a billion Chinese are incapable of participating in this global space as individuals with distinct preferences for labor or environmental or security standards that are no more or less likely to be in tune with their official government positions than those of Canadians or Americans?

One possibility is that the citizens of Third World countries are somehow less individualistic in their democratic choices than their counterparts in the First World. A second, and closer, possibility is that the problem lies in Nye's categories, which continue to be nation-centered—at least as far as the non-Western world is concerned. Since his definitions of the global have not really moved beyond the familiar problematic of the national, the networks turn out, on closer examination, to be fundamentally networks of individuals with preconstituted national identities. Nye's analytical focus thus never truly leaves the space of the international.

Waltz (1999), on the other hand, makes, as I pointed out before, a really useful distinction between interdependence and integration. But he also claims that "with integration, the world would look like one big state." It is one thing to assert, as Waltz correctly does, that markets require governance, but it is a failure of the conceptual imagination to assume that the only form global governance can take is one that it has taken in a particular historical phase. In other words, while he is willing to argue for a qualitative distinction in terms of the economy, he is unable to conceptualize any qualitative change at the level of the polity.

In the end, it is clear that three of the foremost thinkers of rationalist international relations seek, encouragingly, to grasp the production of the global, but their analytical frameworks and conceptual vocabulary serve them poorly as they seek to trace its politics. Much of the problem arises from their a priori neglect of the intersubjectively constituted politics of meaning governing the constitution of the global. They rarely stop to ask: What does the global mean? How are those meanings produced? How are particular shared conceptions of the global institutionalized? Failing in that interpretive task, they fall back on the conventional framework of the international. The politics of the global then gets reduced to the conventional politics of "interdependence," and the rationalist debate about the global becomes yet another site for the recycling of the realist/liberal cant.

CONSTRUCTIVISM

If the main problem with rationalist international relations is its neglect of the meaningful and intersubjective nature of the global, then constructivism, as an approach that emphasizes both meanings and social relations, should be in the best possible position to illuminate the politics of the global. But contemporary constructivism shares the limitations of rationalism in terms of its inability to make space for the intersubjective production of meaning.

John Ruggie's (1982) conceptualization of the post–World War II international economic regime as one of "embedded liberalism" has been an influential and insightful thesis in international political economy. Ruggie's work focused, among other things, on grounding economic processes in their social and political contexts in order to combat an ahistorical economism. The thesis of embedded liberalism did that nicely by showing how the successful expansion of international trade and production was based in important measure on the effective rooting of a compromise among the internal and external obligations of Western capitalist states (1993). Extending that analysis to the contemporary global economy, Ruggie (1994) argued that a series of systematic changes marking the "new world economy" made it qualitatively so different that it could be seen as "disembedded" in important ways. Locating the disembeddedness in three dimensions (the lack of a correlation between the imagined world of policy makers and the existing world, the ineffectivity of policy instruments, and the unraveling of the social compact between domestic society and Western capitalist states), Ruggie deployed the metaphor of home and abroad to signify the shift from an "embedded" to a "disembedded" liberalism.[1]

Ruggie shows us very effectively that important transformations and changes have occurred within a regime that was centered previously on Western capitalist states. A significant part of his argument asserts that this liberalism is now disembedded, that it no longer has a "bed" outside the West. Rather than demonstrating that part of the thesis, however, he leaves it to the reader to assume that this regime that spread its reach beyond Western boundaries is equally "abroad," "not-at-home," or "disembedded" in non-Western and developing states. Whether liberalism is "embedded" or "disembedded" outside Western states is a question that calls for a more interpretive and intersubjective analysis of the historical and spatial interaction between liberalism and the cultural frameworks of non-Western Others. The veracity of his claim cannot even be judged here because Ruggie does not acknowledge or account for that effect in talking about the contemporary politics of the global. What is our basis—other than the unraveling of liberalism from Western sites demarcated as "home"—for claiming that liberalism has not managed to find an alternative "bed" and a "home" outside the boundaries of Western capitalist states? How do we understand this analytical presumption on the part of Ruggie?

Making explicit the uncontested assumptions that govern the discourse of constructivism offers one answer to this question. The disembedding of liberalism outside the spaces of the West can be taken for granted even by the constructivist scholar if the experiences and meanings of those outside it were in some ways either unlikely to make a significant difference to our knowledge of the global or were always already derivable from the temporal experiences of the West: those who inhabit spaces outside the West are either insignificant or experience only what the West has already experienced before. Either way, there is little need to go beyond the boundaries of the West in order to understand the production of the global. Is this a problem of particular constructivist analysts and their analytical choices or something embedded in the conceptual apparatus of constructivism itself? In answering this question, especially as it pertains to constructivism, one must turn to the work of Alexander Wendt.

WENDTIAN CONSTRUCTIVISM

Few scholars have systematized and promoted constructivist analysis as much as Alexander Wendt. His framing of the contemporary debates in international relations around issues of identities and meanings has consistently engaged the rationalists and has been extremely influential. Drawing attention to both social meanings and intersubjectivity, Wendt (1992) also advanced some powerful claims about the mutually constitutive relationship among meanings, identities, and social practices and the process-dependent nature of international institutions and structures. His scholarship offers a useful site for examining the strengths and weaknesses of contemporary constructivism as it pertains to the politics of the global.[2]

Wendtian constructivism presents itself as a "structural theory" of the international system that subscribes to some "core claims" (1994, 385). These core claims inscribe states as the primary units of analysis and posit that the structures of the states system are intersubjectively constructed and that the identities and interests of states are at least partially produced by these structures. Through these claims, however, Wendt makes possible a constructivism that cannot take difference seriously.

Wendt's core claims foreclose any recognition of difference at the level of the primary actors themselves. How, for instance, does the assertion that states are the principal units of analysis follow from constructivist tenets? Constructivism cannot yield such an implication because which realities (and consequently which corresponding social powers) are produced in which spatiotemporal orders cannot be deduced from an approach that assumes that all realities are socially constructed. If anything, constructivism demands that the analyst pay attention to the particular spatiotemporal orders productive of specific social realities.

After assuming that states are the relevant units of analysis, Wendt closes the interpretive space further by postulating certain preexisting identities for these states. He claims that states can be conceptualized as being constituted at two different levels: a corporate level and a social level. A state's corporate identity, Wendt points out, consists of the "intrinsic, self-organizing qualities that constitute actor individuality." It is, he asserts, the equivalent of "the body and experience of consciousness for human beings. In the case of organizations, the corporate identity can be seen as consisting of constituent individuals, physical resources, shared beliefs and institutions in virtue of which individuals function as a 'we'" (1994, 385).

Wendt agrees that "corporate identities have histories" but does not see them as pertinent to his analysis. He justifies this inattention by asserting that "a theory of the states system need no more explain the existence of states than one of society need explain that of people" (1994, 385). Once again, these are troublesome claims to the extent that they close off what they should be engaging: the terrain of the production of social identities. If identities are constitutive of interests and practices, and the corporate identities of states are historical products, shouldn't this historical constitution of state identity be open to meaningful analysis? Wouldn't it have a bearing on what specific identity a state had—at the corporate level—and how it was constitutive of some of its fundamental interests and practices?

Moreover, histories—the stories that states tell themselves about their past—are a function of interpretation, too. They are crucial to understanding what "imagined communities" they reproduce

(Anderson 1991) and what they suffocate. Such issues are, however, bracketed by Wendt. While Wendt does assert (1994, 394 n6) that he does not see corporate identity as "timeless" or "essential," the net effect here is to cordon off any empirical investigation of the historical production of state identities.

The interpretive gap opened up in the understanding of historically imagined state identities is now filled through conceptual fiat by Wendt. Elaborating on the nature of corporate identity, Wendt states that it has "four basic interests or appetites" (1994, 385): first, a need for "physical security, including its differentiation from other actors"; second, a need for "ontological security or predictability in relationships to the world, which creates a desire for stable social identities"; third, a need for "recognition as an actor by others, above and beyond survival through brute force"; and fourth, a need for "development, in the sense of meeting the human aspiration for a better life, for which states are repositories at the collective level."

In addition to a corporate identity with these "basic interests," states also have, according to Wendt, some "social identities" that are "cognitive and structural." They are "the sets of meanings that an actor attributes to itself while taking the perspective of others, that is, as a social object. In contrast to the singular quality of corporate identity, actors normally have multiple social identities that vary in salience. . . . Social identities have both individual and social structural properties, being at once cognitive schemas that enable an actor to determine "who I am/we are" in a situation and positions in a social role structure of shared understandings and expectations" (1994, 385).

Wendt's constructivist theory is limited, therefore, in some very specific ways. By conceptualizing constructivism as a theory rather than as an approach, it implicitly postulates a specific, ahistorical relationship between state identity and state interests, which strongly impedes any empirical analysis beyond that given by the dominant paradigm or the dominant common sense. In specifying what "appetites" states have "basically," Wendt has already established a substantive relationship between corporate identity and interests at one level. Constructivists must now see all state practices as potentially aimed at maintaining a corporate identity with hardwired needs for physical security, ontological security, recognition, and development. This, however, will not be a minor conceptual conces-

sion for constructivists. What is being conceded here—without any empirical validation—is a substantive, historically and culturally specific social identity for states. How so?

Focusing on the conception of a corporate identity, one can ask: What does it mean, for instance, to say that a state has an appetite for or interest in physical security, ontological security, recognition, and development? Such "appetites" are functions of highly context-dependent understandings. For these basic appetites to have analytical power, one must not specify them a priori but engage in concrete historical and empirical research to reconstruct what it is that states historically or culturally understand as their basic interests. Assuming we did so, is there any compelling reason to believe that all states in the world will identify these four interests as their basic ones?

The analytical moment of diversity and difference is arbitrarily closed off here through the positing of a common identity. To take one of the appetites as an illustration, development is not necessarily a given desire for many states. It is only in the spatiotemporal context of modernity that this goal even becomes meaningful for some states (Tomlinson 1991; Sachs 1992). But even after it acquires a certain historical resonance, "development" connotes different things to different states. While Wendt unpacks this desire as "meeting the human aspiration for a better life" (1994, 385), Iran's conception of what this involves might be strikingly different from that of the United States. Such contrasts among states have immense consequences for their identities (corporate and social) and the consequent state practices.

Wendt's attempt to split state identities into two distinct levels only makes sense as an attempt to insulate the corporate identity of states from historical and empirical research. By conceptually legislating what the four basic interests are, Wendt makes it possible for international relations theorists to theorize in systemic terms— about the nature of the interstate system and about how states react to each other—but without soiling their hands through empirical research into the basic interests of historically and culturally embedded states. The constructivist enterprise of taking meanings seriously, showing how identities are constitutive of interests and practices, is now analytically restricted to the level of social identities. At this level, appetites and interests are not postulated but

seen as "always in process during interaction." Social identities are conceded to be multiple and varying in salience and left to empirical analysis to determine.

Thus, Wendt's conceptual distinctions are extremely limiting in terms of empirical analysis. His analytical scheme forces an unhappy choice on constructivists. Accepting his scheme entails accepting a substantive theory of international relations, one that sees states as principal units for analysis and postulates some basic appetites as driving at least one set of state identities. It closes off, theoretically, any analysis of those meaningful differences that should be reconstructed through interpretive analysis. In that sense, as Legro points out in regard to the rationalist treatment of interests, Wendt does a "two-step" of his own in relation to state identities (Legro 1996).

First, state identities (as corporate identity) are formed outside of state interaction, and then the subsequent interactions are treated as if they mattered primarily for social identities. This means that a potentially rich avenue for exploring the culturally and historically varying constitution of state identities and interests is blocked through conceptual legislation. That conceptual legislation is a colonial moment to the extent that it prevents any engagement with the diversity that is productive of the global.

Second, from an empirical point of view, Wendt's constructivism leaves us clueless about how to translate constructivist principles into concrete research projects. In terms of a concrete operationalization, we have two options: accept what the constructivists tell us are a state's basic identities and interests—for example, Wendt's "revelation" of the "basic interests" of states—or take at face value whatever a state declares as its identity or as in its interests. The former option forces us to agree with the theorist's assumptions of state interests; the latter puts us in the position of assuming that a state's identity is whatever it claims it to be. Both options skip the difficult task of how analysts can take social meanings seriously and intersubjectively but without necessarily privileging the views either of the theorists or of the state as the final say on the matter.

Third, the role of "politics" and "power" is not specified clearly within Wendtian constructivism. How are relationships of power imbricated in relations of meanings, identities, and practices? While Wendt refers to the "first" and "third dimensions" of power and distinguishes between "behavioral" and "rhetorical practices" (1994,

391), his primary stress remains on agentic power. The production or transformation of historical and cultural structures through which specific actors are empowered or disempowered as social beings with distinctive social powers is seriously underspecified in Wendt's formulations. As a result, his conceptualizations of how reality is socially constructed remain quite agentic. That in itself is not a problem except insofar as Wendt wants to postulate what that agent's basic identity is across time and space. But a constructivism that is serious about the social production of meaning must also pay attention to the historical and geographical variations in the productions of such meanings. There is little in Wendtian constructivism that lends itself to such a critical orientation. This neglect of the social meanings of those outside the West in the politics of the global is also a feature of some versions of historical-materialist theory.

HISTORICAL MATERIALISM

Historical materialists represent the global as the hegemonic form of the ideology of neoliberalism in the contemporary international system (see Overbeek and Van Der Pijl 1993, 1–2). The ideology of neoliberalism is seen as emerging from the restructuring of world capitalism in the 1980s and understood to be a transnational phenomenon rather than an unrelated series of developments in particular national spaces. Sensitive to historical context and national particularities, historical materialists see neoliberalism as operating with a "different face" in different countries. Understood neither as a coherent economic doctrine nor as an objective knowledge, neoliberalism, within this tradition, is conceptualized as a contradictory set of ideas. Its ideological basis is seen as lying in the fact that its general claims are actually expressive of the parochial interests of a very small group (15).

But how do parochial interests pass themselves off as a general interest? Historical materialists are particularly insightful in drawing attention to the specific politics at play. Drawing a distinction between a "politics of support" and a "politics of power," they locate national variations on the dimension of the "politics of support." The politics of different countries vary based on their historical particularities. Overbeek and Van Der Pijl (1993, 15), for instance, note, "The precise mix of elements (free market ideology and neo-conservatism, destructive and constructive) varies from country to country, depending on the political conjuncture and the country's particular place in the world order of the 1970s." This important concession frees up space for an explicit acknowledgment of historical and geographical difference in the production of the global. Other actors and places are not mere victims but, potentially, agents in their own right.

Compared to rationalist theories, historical-materialist explanations are more self-conscious about their conceptual relationships. Overbeek and Van Der Pijl (1993), for example, argue that three conceptual "problematics" have long united discussions in historical-materialist international relations. The first is the "'internal-external' dialectic" of capitalism, which focuses on the relations that operate between global capitalism and domestic economic developments. The second is that of "territorial non-coincidence," which deals with the increasing disjuncture between the "territorial reach" of capital and the boundaries of the nation-state. The third, that of structure and agency, involves a specification of the mutually constitutive relationships between the logics of capital and the practices of the bourgeoisie.

Though quite nuanced when it comes to an analysis of complexities of neoliberalism in the West, many historical materialists also relapse into simplistic narratives when it comes to spaces outside the West. This is evident in a number of ways but most of all in the assumption that states, spaces, and identities outside the West are generally imperfect versions of the Western capitalist state (see, for example, Van Der Pijl 1993). That this is not accidental but systematic in the historical materialism of international relations is evident when one analyzes the standard historical-materialist text on global political economy.[3]

Stephen Gill and David Law's classic work, *The Global Political Economy* (1988), lays out the basic principles of the historical-materialist, specifically neo-Gramscian, approach to issues of international political economy.[4] As a substantive tradition, neo-Gramscian political economy is organized primarily around the production and demise of a U.S.-centered hegemonic world order—Pax Americana—from 1945 to about the early 1970s. This hegemonic order was structured around the compromise of embedded liberalism in Western capitalist countries and based on Fordist production practices and on the material, normative, and strategic dominance of the United States in a Cold War world.

Neo-Gramscians such as Gill also read the new global economy as the gradual coming to hegemony of a specific transnational class with a particular ideology of disciplinary neoliberalism. The Gramscian conceptualization of hegemony allows theorists within this tradition to see the workings of this ideology as containing elements of both coercion and consent. Their conceptualization of the constant interaction between changes in material capabilities, ideas, and institutions at three different analytic levels allows them to integrate conceptually the role of various social forces, social meanings, and social identities in the production of hegemony.[5] More important, it allows them to point to the ways in which cultural knowledge and ideas as intersubjective meanings work to bring about changes in state identities and to transform domestic policies.

Notwithstanding the conceptual self-consciousness and the historically specific analyses—and without taking away from the merit of the overall scholarship—the larger historical-materialist story is always already foretold in theory.[6] While individual concepts vary—classes, fractions of capital, historic blocs, social forces, productive practices, organic intellectuals, ideologies—they always come together in the end, in one form or another—as material and normative structures, regimes of accumulation, or hegemonic world orders—to tell the story of the rise, fall, and rise of Western capitalism.

An international system scripted on this logic appears to be open to the experiences of non-Western communities and spaces in terms of their different cultural understandings and appropriations of history. Any historic bloc, for instance, needs the coming together of a set of social meanings, social forces, and material capabilities that are heavily context, and hence country, dependent. A historic bloc in the Malaysian context is not necessarily the same as a historic bloc in the U.S. context, and thus one cannot easily be derived or read from the other. This makes neo-Gramscian political economy apparently open to agency, meanings, and experiences of developing states. That turns out to be an illusory promise because, openness to the experiences of other states notwithstanding, the narrative of neo-Gramscian political economy rarely trespasses into social realities where Western capitalism is not the driving force of historical changes.

Measured against a history with a metropolitan motor, non-Western states always appear as incomplete projects, as lacks awaiting fulfillment. Note, for example, Gill and Law's analysis of India's economic strategy after independence:

> In countries like India, nationalist and socialist ideas were fused. Nationalist ideas favored the growth of military spending and the establishment of arms production. State-sponsored military-industrial development often became a feature of some less-developed countries. This was sometimes based on the application of the Soviet model of central planning. It has been associated with a state capitalist class. However, this may be a transitional phase, reflecting the backwardness of some countries where, at independence, a bourgeoisie was largely lacking. (1988, 97)

The cultural meanings constitutive of states such as India appear here primarily as a fusion of nationalist and socialist ideas as if these were unproblematically different and easily separable elements, already given from elsewhere, and not constitutive in fundamental ways of an identity such as "India." Their teleology of development fixes the "less-developed" state at a particular stage in a history with the developed West as its vanguard. The absent bourgeoisie and the transitional phase testify to the "incompleteness" of the developing state, a "lack" awaiting completion, which arises primarily because non-Western states are defined, framed, and judged within a framework of categories that takes the Western experience as the universal norm. Such a framework does great violence to the heterogeneous social meanings and the diversity of historical experiences constitutive of the global. It ignores the need to take seriously the different meanings, social myths, and cultural self-understandings constitutive of state and national identities.[7]

Historical materialists present a script where a capitalism that had its historical origins in Europe meets a variety of Others—racial, sexual, gender, caste-differentiated subjects—that offer varying degrees of cooperation or resistance to its overall project of perpetual accumulation. But those who are different never manage to quite master this process or overwrite its goals. While much is generously given to these others, they are always denied History. History is never the history of these different Others—of Religion, Race, Nation, Gender, Caste, or Power, for example—but always the continuous and universal, even if uneven, development of Capital (e.g., Kolko 1988, 350).

COLONIAL DISCOURSES AND THE POLITICS OF MEANING

Omar, an Iraqi fifteen-year-old, is an orphan today because those who wanted to "liberate" him, acting under some problematic assumptions about Others in the world, ended up killing his father, mother, two of his sisters, a brother, and an uncle.[8] Faced with a situation of ignorance ("We didn't know what was in that bus"), they assumed the universality of their language ("Everyone understands the word 'stop,' right?"). That combination of ignorance and what Todorov (1999, 42–43) calls "egocentrism" ("the identification of our own values with values in general, of our *I* with the universe—in the conviction that the world is one") was backed with deadly coercive force and a particular choice about their preferred ethical relationship to the Other ("It may sound bad, but I'd rather see more of them dead than any of my friends").

Hochschild's narrative itself is not free from such egocentric assumptions. He equates (1998, 3), all too easily, his ignorance with the ignorance of *the world*, or is surprised that his education did not inscribe the Congo's horrors into the "standard litany of our century's horrors." But it is not a Todorovian egocentrism that alone is the problem here. It is also the capacity of the self to hide from itself the primary source of the problem: the inability or unwillingness of the colonizer/liberator to "escape from himself" (Todorov 1999, 41) in its dealings with the Other and to establish a relationship that is more intersubjective than colonial.

Narratives of international relations, for all their provinciality, come, like the marines, from sites endowed with immense coercive power. If they want to establish an ethically defensible engagement with diverse Others in the world, they need to remember, acknowledge, and explore the epistemological implications of their historically colonial nature.

2

Critical Constructivism

Groups of 250 to 300 teenagers hurled stones at Marines patrolling the holy city of Najaf, south of the capital, in two separate incidents on Thursday and Friday, officers said. . . . Marines said their translators had told them that in one case the crowd had mistaken them for British troops, against whom they have grievances dating to colonial times in the first half of the 20th century—a sobering lesson for the Americans about how long memories are in Iraq.

NADIM LADKI, *REUTERS*

"To think globality," observes Gayatri Chakravorty Spivak "is to think the politics of thinking globality" (1999, 364). The conventional politics of thinking globality in the social sciences and humanities operates, by and large, on the terrain of categories and frameworks drawn from the provincial experience of Europe and its modernity (Chakrabarty 2001). International relations is no exception to this trend (Inayatullah and Blaney 2001; Krishna 2001, 1999). Equally clearly, as postcolonial theorists remind us, the globality that we inhabit allows us no pure non-European or non-Western positions from which to engage in this enterprise. Any analysis of the global must now necessarily work in a framework within which Europe is both "inadequate" and "indispensable" (Chakrabarty 2001). I wish to approach the production of the global in ways that acknowledge the possibility of its multiple meanings even as I recognize that power privileges the materialization of only some of those. What are the conceptual implications of such a perspective for constructivist approaches?

Constructivism offers the basic insight that reality is socially produced. Given the diversity of human beings and political communities in the world, it is reasonable to assume that there are multiple social realities, multiple ways of imagining and inhabiting our world. If so, how should we think of the global in such a multiply interpretable world?

I propose that globality involves two minimal processes that can be treated distinctly for our purposes: the constitution of a shared understanding of what "the global" is from among multiple imaginations and the "real-ization" of this specific imagination of the global over/against alternative imaginations. Relations of multiple meanings, intersubjectivity, and power are thus intricately involved in the interpretive constitution and material realization of the global from among many possible ones. My separation of the meaningful and the material is only an analytical one.

The constructivist insight that realities are multiply constituted and realized does not rule out the possibility that some ways of imagining and realizing the world may be better than others on various socially shared criteria. What it does, though, is to point out that such criteria are human choices that are intersubjectively negotiated and also necessarily political. They are thus contested normative principles, not divinely revealed subjective pronouncements or objective truths standing outside of any interpretive challenge. In other words, I am not interested in claiming that every form of globality is equally desirable just because all forms of globality are intersubjectively constructed and involve various relations of power. What matters are the political principles implicit in the constitution and institutionalization of particular systems of globality.

Given a multiply imagined and inhabited world, any constitution and institutionalization of the global must implicitly or explicitly involve a social negotiation of difference—at the level of imaginations, identities, and interests. Based on the normative principles governing the negotiation of difference, I posit two polar models of globality: a colonial globality structured around the silencing of difference and a postcolonial one that relates to difference through democratic engagement and dialogue.

In colonial globalities, the production of the global lacks an intersubjective dimension and never really engages the Other. As an extension to Others of the discourse of the Self, colonial representations of the global rely on coercive power—the capacity to inflict violence and/or control the conditions of living—to be effective.[1] In such conditions, it is often only counterviolence that opens up a space for the acknowledgment of difference. Postcolonial globalities are structured on the acknowledgment of and respect for diversity and democracy. The productions of the global in postcolonial globalities are polylogical and conducive to mutual transformations of diverse realities, identities, and interests.

One implication, of the perspective outlined above, is that critical constructivism must extend its analytical realm to include the often taken-for-granted production of dominant and subordinate social realities, including the reality of distinctively understood spatiotemporal orders that generate political effects at the level of political and economic spaces and the identities of social actors reproduced within such spaces. They do this by empowering the social identities and social powers of some actors while denying the social identities and powers of others.

A second implication that follows for a critical constructivism is that answers to questions about the strategies and practices of specific actors, such as states, might lie in the realm of the social identities produced as dominant within different spatiotemporal orders. If reality is socially constructed and there are different constructions of reality, it would be theoretically productive to explore the nature of such different constructions, the ways in which they relate to each other, and the causal influence they have on the generation of specific social identities and social powers. Though politics permeates the whole process, I am particularly interested in the politics involved in the interactions between different social realities as they are productive of the distinctive identities and powers constitutive of states and economies and the nature of the relations governing their mutual interaction.

ON CONCEPTS: INTERESTS, PREFERENCES, AND SOCIAL CLAIMS

In mainstream international relations, the category of "interests" (national interest, self-interest) provides a prominent way of understanding the practices of states and other social agents, but it is never really clear how the analyst establishes what the interests governing an agent's action are. The relevant interests must be inferred by the analyst by tracing what the actor's preferences (as expressed in specific actions) are assumed to reveal. If a state initiates a process of globalization, the analyst assumes that it had a preference for it. Imputing a rationality to the state, the analyst works backward from that action to discover the ways in which that action could come about at that particular moment. While justified as elegant and parsimonious, this method employs the assumption of rationality fairly loosely (very few actions can be seen as irrational on this basis) and privileges whatever action is undertaken as somehow expressing the preferences (the goals, desires, interests) of the actor.

Against this mainstream concept, I would argue for conceptualizing interests through a more interpretive concept: *social claims*. Social claims are unit-level concepts that are definitionally relational. Defined as individual demands, obligations, and self-understandings, social claims furnish analysts with a way to conceptualize an agent's actions as they relate to the actions of other units. When an agent demands something, expresses certain interests, sees herself as obligated in some ways, or understands herself, those demands, obligations, or understandings are necessarily, if implicitly, in relation to someone or something else. She is demanding something *of* someone, sees herself as obligated *to* someone, or understands herself in relation *to* someone else or something else.[2]

This concept, even as it presents an agent's actions, necessarily presents that action in some specific social relationship to others. The concept is relational in that it acquires meaning only in its connection to another term: another agent, thing, entity, or object. To the extent that the demands, obligations, and self-understandings of the individual unit are seen as *social* claims, society always provides the implicit context that is invoked to generate meaning.

Preferences, as a concept, are not relational in the sense that social claims are. With preferences, the analyst is not forced to take the socially produced and interpretive dimension seriously. She does not need to know where the agent's preferences come from, how they acquire meaning, why they make sense to the agent, or how and why they change. There is no necessary connection posited to the social. The analytical choice is limited to accepting the agent's rationale for engaging in an action or inferring what an ideal rational actor would have done in that particular situation. The former completely privileges the subjective viewpoint of the actor, allowing anything and everything to become rational just because the actor thought so. The latter results in the analyst substituting her judgment of what was objectively rational for the meaningful claims of the agent. This is equally problematic since the social context determining the analyst's assumption of rationality might not be that of the agent in question. There is no way, in this tradition, to move from the dichotomous choice of the subjective or the seemingly objective to the socially meaningful world of the intersubjective.

Social claims, on the other hand, cannot even be adequately defined if they stop with the subjective world of the individual. The social claims of any agent make sense only when they are situated in their appropriate social context. That is, sociality is built into the conceptualization of the individual's action itself. By specifying "social" as the term to which "claims" must always be joined to, the concept postulates an analytical need to constantly reconstruct the social context.

Consider certain universals such as human rights, freedom, democracy, and liberation. Such desirable interests are often supported by asserting their basis in a global morality that seemingly transcends politics, context, and issues of agency and social power. Any attempt to locate these in a particular historical or social context is immediately problematized as either a sign of relativism or cultural bigotry.

This conceptual space empowers, for example, Senator John McCain's claim that the United States is unlike other "empire builders" because it deploys its "power for moral purpose." This also allows him to assert that "'Experts' who dismiss hopes for Iraqi democracy . . . do not explain why they believe Iraqis or Arabs are uniquely unsuited for representative government, and they betray a cultural bigotry that ill serves our interests and values."[3] McCain's claim implies that there is a theoretically pure way of establishing a global morality in a world characterized by a diversity of political communities. Global moral values are not precluded but dependent on their endorsement by significant sections of those communities. But opportunities for bringing in the voices and the meaningfulness of the claims of the Others are ruled out in this case by accusations of cultural bigotry.

Better possibilities open up if such universals are conceptualized as social claims that human beings make and expect recognition of from one another. Their best justification then is not that these demands are somehow objective or rooted in some incontrovertible global morality but that they are intersubjectively desirable and socially constituted. This means that it is politically desirable to work toward a situation where the mutual acknowledgment of human rights and democracy is socially and legally empowered.

Working toward such a goal might mean an active engagement with those Others who have alternative conceptions of seemingly global morals (democracy, liberation, and freedom). An awareness of the social context of claims is thus analytically helpful in engaging with difference in a world that is multiply interpretable and inhabitable. But it is ethically and politically very powerful, too, since it provides a shared terrain to construct alliances and to resolve political differences that arise from different understandings of social realities. What it is not conducive to is the unilateral and colonial assertion of one's preferences as the preferences of the world.

The assumption of human agency also implies that while society is an ever-present and necessary condition of the meanings of various social claims, it is never completely determinative of them. Thus, social claims allow us to capture the agentic aspect of human actions without sacrificing their sociality. Actors can therefore be seen as functioning in society by constantly making claims on each other and by understanding, acknowledging, rearticulating, or denying each others' claims. What these social claims are, how well they are understood or misunderstood, how symmetrically they are distributed in terms of acknowledgments or denials might differ in space and time. What is undeniable, though, is that we function socially through the recognition of mutual claims. A situation where no claim whatsoever was understood or acknowledged by human beings on each other is a situation where society is nonexistent.

SOCIAL IMAGINARIES

The question then is not so much if social claims are present as what sort of social claims are understood, acknowledged, and implicitly or explicitly empowered in particular spatiotemporal orders. In acknowledging or denying various sets of social claims, any field of social claims structures social identities, social powers, and the political space of action by social actors. While critical, such a structuring is not a one-way street such that only the field of social claims is productive of the identities and social powers of actors. The set of social claims themselves are constantly either transformed or reproduced through the actions of social actors. This means that the field of social claims exists in a mutually constitutive relationship with the social identities and the actors it is productive of.

Given the diversity of societies in the international system, it is not difficult to see that a variety of historical and social processes are constitutive of distinctive fields of social claims. The analyst has to find a way of capturing the central structuring principles that are productive of the mutually constitutive relationship between collectively meaningful but diverse social claims and specific identities, interests, and practices. Central structuring principles draw our attention to the boundaries—the inside/outside relations—that are constitutive of spatiotemporally distinctive fields of social claims.

The concept of *social imaginaries* allows the analyst to capture the complex but mutually constitutive relationship that exists between specific social claims and the distinctive social identities and inside/outside relations that they generate. Adapting from the work of Castoriadis (1987), I conceptualize social imaginaries as distinctive fields of meanings and social power. Operating as a field of meanings, the social imaginary provides an organized set of interpretations—or social claims—for making sense of a complex world. Operating as a field of social power, the social imaginary works to produce specific relations of power through the production of distinctive social identities. My analytical separation notwithstanding, both operations are moments of the same process.

The social imaginary is thus constitutive of a set of organized interpretations and social identities simultaneously. The social identities that are reproduced by the social imaginary cannot be specified a priori but can be established through a reconstruction of the sets of meanings operating within it. The social imaginary exists in a mutually productive relationship with social actors and is thus either reproductive or transformative of their social identities and relatedly their powers, interests, and practices.

The imaginary, within this conception, refers to the structuring principles underlying the set of meanings and social relations and constituting them into specific social identities. The imaginary, in this sense, is a social signification that is prior to our conceptions of reality and rationality (Castoriadis 1987; Tomlinson 1991). To that extent, it is the key to understanding the distinctive representations of social reality that are productive of various social identities and practices. The discursive boundaries of the social imaginary are reached when particular representations of the world seem meaningless and specific practices appear strange or irrational within the reality produced by the imaginary.

One of the primary ways in which the social imaginary operates is by its capacity to organize and institutionalize the sets of meanings through which agents understand the world and act within it. Social claims are subsets of such understandings. The institutionalization of meanings by social imaginaries is simultaneously productive or transformative of existing social identities and powers. The social organization of meanings works as a political process in at least two ways through mechanisms such as articulation and interpellation (Hall 1985, 1988; Laclau 1977; Althusser 1971).

Articulation can be understood, at a minimum, as the establishment of certain compelling links between different elements of meaning. This process makes sense with the assumption that there is no intrinsically necessary connection between different elements of meaning and that the arrangement between such elements is conventional but not logically given. "Kentucky Fried Chicken," in the American context, has associations with fried chicken and fast food. In the Indian context, the same term has associations with imperialism, westernization, and modernity. The social meanings of the term "Kentucky Fried Chicken" are a function of the other social meanings it is linked to or articulated with and the social relations and identities such meanings are productive of. What the resultant economic practices of social actors are—whether the product is consumed for its inexpensiveness and convenience (as in the United States) or for its expensiveness and difference from the ordinary lifestyles of millions of others (as in India), whether the restaurant is able to sell its products and make profits or is frequently ransacked and forced to shut down—depends largely on the social meanings and relations that are empowered by the specific social imaginary.

Articulations are thus political mechanisms produced within a social imaginary. Their production and reproduction involves political struggles over which combinations of social meanings are legitimate and which are illegitimate. Such political struggles involve implicit and explicit claims and contestations over social identities involving, among other things, existing imaginings of personal and community identities.

Social agents, however, are not dupes waiting to be swayed by different articulations of social meanings. As amateur social theorists, they appropriate and reorganize sets of available meanings to structure their lived realities and to function effectively within it. For these reasons the analyst cannot take it for granted that because specific articulations are made or exist within the social imaginary, they are also received and reproduced unproblematically by the audience.

The concept of *interpellation* helps us check the reception of these meanings by social actors (Althusser 1971). Interpellation refers to the ways in which actors respond to being socially claimed in specific ways. For the analyst, interpellation is a useful window into the question of how persuasive some social claims are to social actors. Do they resonate to these articulations? Do they recognize themselves in them? Does it help them make sense of complex and uncertain social realities? If an articulatory claim is met by an interpellatory response, then articulations and interpellations mutually confirm each other. In doing this, they set up "reciprocating circles of meanings and social powers"[4] that generate specific social identities with distinctive social powers, interests, and practices.

It is not enough, for instance, for some citizens to proclaim that KFC is a foreign company that is out to exploit countries such as India. Their articulation of specific meanings—of "foreign" against "Indian," of "exploitation" against "development"—must resonate with the intended audience. If that is effective, it results in the generation of identities that define their national identity against the foreignness of KFC. But it is not just personal social identities that are generated. At stake also are renegotiations of the existing boundaries of national and other spaces and identities: what is Indian against what is Western, what is domestic against what is foreign. Such renegotiations have consequences for the social powers of actors such as other foreign companies and economic processes such as the inflow of foreign direct investment.

Contestations abound over the appropriate meanings and boundaries of such social claims and involve political struggles over identities, interests, and practices. Articulation and interpellation are thus also claim-making and claim-acknowledging mechanisms that illuminate the institutionalization of meanings and the production of identities within and through a social imaginary.

ANALYZING THE POLITICS OF THE GLOBAL

I have dealt, so far, with the importance of the interpretive and inter-subjective dimensions in any analysis of the politics of the global. To facilitate this task, I have argued for a critical constructivism that is conceptually equipped to explore these dimensions. I have also sought to demonstrate how the concepts of social claims, so-cial imaginaries, articulation, and interpellation are not only better than the conventional concepts of interests, preferences, system, and structure, but also offer critical constructivists insightful ways of examining the production of the global.

The production of the global is a systemic phenomenon that nec-essarily has a mutually constitutive relationship with the situated practices of social actors. In that sense, the systemic production of the global, frequently conceptualized as globalization, is not outside of individual actors but is constantly reproduced or transformed through their identities, meanings, and practices. Any empirical analysis of globalization must therefore examine the embedded prac-tices of specifically situated social actors to see how their actions are either productive or transformative of this systemic phenomenon.

Keeping that in view, I focus my subsequent analysis of the pro-duction of the global very deliberately on two crucial nation-states in the international system. My empirical analysis seeks to reconstruct how their economic and security practices are empowered and dis-empowered by their location in certain historically institutionalized national spaces. After examining the ways in which these practices are made sense of by these states, I examine whether the different interpretations are productive or transformative of the global.

WHY INDIA AND THE UNITED STATES?

A combination of reasons lie behind my choice of these two states. First and foremost, an important aspect of globalization has been the emergence of strong flows between seemingly disjunctured and unlikely national spaces (Appadurai 1996). The flow of Indian com-puter software professionals and doctors into the United States, the establishment of outsourcing facilities, back offices, and call centers in India to cater to the needs of American corporations and customers, the flow of remittances and diasporic capital from nonresident Indians in the United States back into India, the attempts of many Indian cities to replicate the success of the United States' Silicon Valley model of development, the serious consideration of dual citizenship by India—all speak to the emergence of distinctively powerful Indo-U.S. economic flows.

Such economic flows have been complemented in recent years by the increasing coordination of security practices across the world by these two states. From support for the United States' missile defense plan to its stance on the International Criminal Court, Indo-U.S. security cooperation has been growing steadily. What makes the emergence of these flows so surprising and worthy of exploration is their historical anomalousness. Indo-U.S. relations were highly insecure during the Cold War, primarily because of a strong disjuncture in their social imaginaries (Muppidi 1999). Clearly, the emergence of these new flows has been facilitated by a rearticulation of the dominant social meanings productive of these two spaces.

Someone else, with a different background, could probably make a similar argument in the case of Sino-U.S. relations, more so given the amount of U.S. investment in China. It would be against the spirit of this study to deny such connections. My primary analytical claim so far, however, has been the importance of deeply intersubjective and interpretive accounts of the global. I do see myself, and many of my generation of Indians, as one of the products of such Indo-U.S. flows. That, I believe, allows me an immersion and associated sense of relative interpretive competency in reading both spaces. This immersion, more than anything else, drives me to focus on the production of the global in and through Indo-U.S. encounters.

3

Globalization in India

India's renewed integration into the global economy began in 1991. Writing about Indian economic reforms, Raja Chelliah, an economist prominently associated with the globalization of the Indian economy, noted, "Under the new policy regime, economics comes into its own" (1996, 5). Pointing to "the globalization of national economies, the strong growth performance of several countries, and the emergence of large trading blocks," he claimed that economics now prevailed over politics and "old style diplomacy" (1). An understanding of the contemporary world as one where the economic prevails over the political is the dominant perspective of many who support the continued "liberalization" of the Indian economy.[1]

Pursuing the primacy of the economic over the political requires, they argue, that economic considerations be given explicit recognition and adequate weight in the formulation of Indian economic policy. Implicit here is the subtext that much of Indian economic policy, especially in its broad insulation of the Indian economy from the international one, was based on political considerations. This call to give higher priority to the economic also goes hand in hand with the subsidiary claim that India's liberalization should be based on the "scientific" knowledge that the discipline provides them about the workings of economies globally. Many of the "distortions" in the Indian economy, they point out, can be rectified by the knowledge available from this outside realm: the realm of economic reason as generated from the theory and experience of successful economies in the contemporary world. The realm of the economic is implicitly the domain of the global while the realm of the political is that of the local. Indian globalization, on this account, is also its liberation from the world of local politics into the world of global economic reason.

Jagdish Bhagwati, a leading economist and proponent of reforms, expresses this epistemological privilege (and frustration with fellow economists who believe otherwise) very well when he observes, "Many of my non-Indian economist friends who have visited India confess to astonishment that in India, virtually alone among the world's developing nations, there are still trained economists who doubt and even oppose, as against leading reforms" (1998, 24 n1). From Bhagwati's perspective, something about being trained as an economist should automatically place one on the side of liberalizing the Indian economy rather than opposing it. To be different, to be otherwise, to oppose reforms after being trained as an economist is to be an anomaly to the economists of the world.

It is important to note that many proponents of Indian economic liberalization are not crude admirers of the magic of the market. They are quite conversant with and frequently explicit about the limitations of their domain of expertise and also of modifications required by the particularities of the Indian economy (e.g., Chelliah 1996, 16–18). Notwithstanding that qualification, they see the liberalization of the Indian economy as primarily a technical issue and not one that is in itself political. Politics comes in from the outside as the specific compulsions of policy makers and in the implementation of these reforms.

Situating themselves within this domain of economic expertise, proponents of Indian economic reforms have offered various reasons for how and why India should liberalize its economy. Typically, these prescriptions have focused on increasing the rate of growth in the Indian economy by removing internal distortions, making more efficient use of internal resources, facilitating the increased participation of private actors, and changing the nature of state intervention from direct control to indirect governance. In terms of relations with those outside the national space, they call for a greater hospitality toward private foreign capital. They have, more than anything else, called for a changed definition of the historically institutionalized meanings of Indian "self-reliance," tracing many of the problems in the Indian economy to what they see as an incorrect understanding of it. Self-reliance, they argue, should be understood not as minimizing the nation's reliance on others in the world but as the generation of an internal capacity to pay for what one secures from the outside. This necessitates increasing exports to others in the world and thus a necessarily more "competitive" self (Chelliah 1996, 6).

Despite a widespread effort by policy makers to present Indian economic liberalization as primarily an issue of technically desirable changes, opponents of the process have insisted on politicizing it as an issue of national identity. Economics, in that sense, has found it extremely difficult to "come into its own." The debate on India's economic liberalization has rarely been confined to technical issues. It has quite often strayed, even among the economists, into questions about the nature of the Indian self, about Indian national identity, and about the desirable relation to the rest of the world, particularly the West. By tracing the negotiations of these social meanings and of the contours of this straying, one can detect the politics of the global in India.

SOCIAL CLAIMS

Indian policy makers have tried, insistently, to articulate economic reforms as primarily a technical issue. P. V. Narasimha Rao, the prime minister who initiated Indian economic reforms, claimed that the primary goal of the new policy was "to accelerate technological change and modernize the Indian economy in order to make it efficient and internationally competitive" (1995, 87). These economic reforms, he declared, did not involve any change in long-standing national goals. They were only a change in methods (112).

Rao's articulation of economic reforms as a technical issue of efficiency, modernization, and competitiveness was not a very successful enterprise initially. The debate over economic reforms was marked by strong denunciations of the economic reformers as people who had mortgaged India's "economic sovereignty," a charge seen as grave enough to merit a categorical denial by the prime minister in Parliament (Rao 1995, 112). The finance minister, accused of acting under the dictates of the International Monetary Fund (IMF), was offended enough to submit his resignation to the prime minister.[2] Rao's statements were thus not very effective in hailing their audience.

Prominent in the opposition, many Marxist economists did not necessarily disagree with the criticisms of the post-independent Indian economic regime. They engaged the technical claims of the reformers but in the wider context of their understanding of the broader capitalist economy. Their greatest criticism of liberalization centered on reading it as a political move away from the process of the Indian nation's continued decolonization.

Prabhat Patnaik (1998), a well-known Marxist economist and critic of the reforms, argued, for instance, that though India pursued capitalist development after independence, it was for the purpose of greater autonomy from "metropolitan capital." But the new economic policies represented a move away from that independence insofar as they diminished the Indian state's control over the national economy and oriented it to the interests of external actors. This increased responsiveness to external actors, he argued, would lead to domestic policies that served "international rentier" interests primarily and those of the nationals secondarily. Such a development, Patnaik noted, also had the potential to negate the technical goals of economic reform, such as increased growth and greater efficiency in the use of resources. Rather than prioritizing technical issues, Patnaik argued for a greater political effort on the part of the Indian state to bring about certain crucial domestic changes—land reforms, industrial policy—that would allow it to retain its "autonomy of decision-making."

Following a broadly similar line of thinking, the Communist Party of India (Marxist) has frequently protested that Indian economic reforms mortgage the economy and fail to protect the interests as well as the economic sovereignty of the country.

What is the conceptualization of the global here? In Patnaik's analysis, the national inside is the space of regulation and autonomy, a controlled area. The world outside India is interpreted primarily as a constraint, as a space outside the Indian state's control but peopled by more powerful interests such as international rentiers. The Indian state is understood to be mediating the relationship between the national and the international with some degree of internal autonomy in decision making. In this context, liberalization is articulated as a process that would make the state more responsive to the outside, threaten its internal autonomy, and hurt its capacity to look after domestic interests. The global appears primarily as a constraint on the national and on the ability of the state to control this national space rather than as an opportunity or as a space that has the potential to increase the state's powers or overall autonomy. Such a conceptualization is not limited to the left but is also shared by some on the other side of the Indian political spectrum—although they arrive at it through a different articulation.

The Swadeshi Jagaran Manch (SJM), affiliated to the ruling Hindu nationalist Bharatiya Janata Party (BJP), has been a consistent critic of Indian liberalization, seeing it as a loss of the nation's sovereignty. Like the Marxists, the SJM sees the global as a strong danger to the autonomy of the Indian nation and state. Unlike the Marxists, it places its faith not on the state but on what it conceptualizes as India's national culture. Economic liberalization, for the SJM, is a dangerously flawed process because it believes that a weak Indian state is not equipped to correctly handle the dangers posed by the outside. The Indian state lacks self-confidence because it is not representative of the authentic culture of the Indian nation. Only when the true representatives of this "swadeshi" culture—defined as that "which is natural and native to a country and society, but allows scope for assimilation of wholesome and beneficial elements from the outside"— lead the state can India liberalize without any dangers. Thus, political parties of the left and the right both opposed Indian liberalization but through different articulations.[3] Both were united in refusing to concede any primacy to economics over politics. The left privileged politics as the autonomy of the state over specific social forces, while the right privileged national culture over the state and the economy.

Other public voices expressed similar concerns. Some feared that liberalization would swamp India with Western commodities and values. The SJM articulated such fears but so did many other social movements, such as the Narmada Bachao Andolan (Save the Narmada Movement) and the Karnataka Rajya Raitha Sangha (KRRS, Karnataka Farmers Association).[4] Medha Patkar, the coordinator of the National Alliance of Peoples' Movements (NAPM), called on Indians to boycott the commodities of multinational corporations and proposed that "the country quit the World Trade Organisation and campaign for an alternative institution to regulate world trade in a democratic, pro-people and environmentally sustainable way." Liberalization was seen as a process that would "deprive people of control over resources and security of food and livelihood."[5]

Patkar speaks not in the name of an essential Indian culture or of the autonomous state but in the name of the "people." It is tempting to think of the NAPM as offering a perspective of the nation from below as against the state's view of the nation from above. A more careful reading of their program, however, reveals a conceptualization of the people as an open-ended set of concrete groups (e.g., Dalits, Adivasis, fisherfolk, peasants, agricultural and industrial laborers, women and youth) that are affected negatively by "development." What unites them is their desire to resist the dominant model of development.

What is their conception of the dangers from globalization? One could say that the NAPM seeks to counter two "outsides." Within the space of the nation, it resists the encroachments of a mainstream society that in the name of modernity and development forces change on already integrated human communities without their consent or participation and against their interests.[6] In this conception, mainstream values are not the values of the people, at least not those of the "toilers." The second outside is constituted by various multinational corporations and global institutions (the World Bank, IMF, WTO) that promote the dominant conception of development. Against the primacy of technical economics of the reformers and the international institutions, the NAPM posits an economics and politics of the people. It does not necessarily want to prevent change as much as to empower the recipients of these changes as full-fledged participants in that process.

When the government first initiated economic restructuring in 1991, many prominent industrialists in India banded together as the Bombay Club to argue for what they called a level playing field for Indian industry. Barely a few years after economic reforms—and a variety of other social claims that posited Indian industrialists as the biggest gainers from these new economic policies—many industrialists continued to complain about foreign multinationals. In March 1995, the Confederation of Indian Industry (a leading supporter of economic restructuring) stunned the Indian government by strongly criticizing the activities of multinational corporations (MNCs) in India.[7] By and large, Indian industrialists have subscribed to a view that, notwithstanding globalization, the Indian state should acknowledge that "capital has color" and protect its industrialists.[8] Those who have welcomed liberalization have seen it as liberating them primarily from the watch of government bureaucrats. They were finally, as one of them claimed, their "own masters" (128).[9]

I have reconstructed various voices in the Indian debate over globalization to show that not only are there multiple articulations of what it means but also that these articulations have rarely been limited, against the best efforts of the government, to technical issues of economic expertise. The negotiation of the various meanings of liberalization has taken place on the terrain of the nature of the Indian state, Indian culture, Indian people, or Indian capital. Far from coming into its own, economics has been consistently subordinated to the social meanings of the Indian nation. How should one understand this dominance of the national over the economic? How does this dominance affect the politics of the global in the Indian case? Answering these questions requires a brief digression into the social imaginary productive of the Indian nation.

THE INDIAN SOCIAL IMAGINARY

India broke free from British colonialism in 1947. Jawaharlal Nehru, India's first prime minister, voiced that historical rupture with India's colonial past:

> A moment comes but rarely in history, when we step out from the old to the new, when an age ends, and when the soul of a nation, long suppressed, finds utterance. . . . We end today a period of ill fortune and India discovers herself again. (1961, 13)

This was India's moment of sovereignty and self-discovery: from this moment on India was finally free, Indians governed themselves, and Indians were responsible for their own actions in history. Given this break with the past and this transition from "the old to the new," one could expect this new beginning to signify a complete break with the legacy of colonialism. A new India, one could reasonably claim, would be manifestly discontinuous with the old, colonial India of the British Empire. Was there such a clean and total break with the nonsovereign, colonial past? Was post-independence India one that had completely repudiated its colonial legacy?

Two factors spoil such a neat transformation from a colonial status to a completely decolonized one. First, the historical legacy of the nationalist struggle meant that the vision of an independent India had been in the imagining in the social and cultural space before being empowered politically through the apparatus of the state (Chatterjee 1986). In other words, the social meanings of the nation had been imagined into cultural existence long before the power of the state was mobilized in its service. Such an imagining of India was only possible—given the historical imbrication of the Indian nation within the British Empire (the "jewel in the crown")—through specific cultural work that repudiated the British connection in various ways. That is, the nationalist movement had to struggle—through contestatory social claims—to establish viable and persuasive articulations that differentiated the Indian nation (the Self) from the British Empire (the Other). The cultural imagining of the Indian nation thus had a lengthy history that predated its specific juridical empowerment.

Second, the nationalist leaders who came to power did not disavow all the colonial institutions that they inherited but utilized them in the governance of independent India. The colonial Indian Civil Service continued on as the Indian Administrative Service, though with the new mission of developing Indian society and economy rather than overseeing it as before. The political leadership relied significantly on an inherited colonial police and on an economic regulatory apparatus bequeathed by the British. It did not sever all its external links with the British (colonial) Empire even though specific political control had passed into Indian hands. The army was nationalized primarily in the sense that British officials were gradually replaced and control passed into Indian hands (Ministry of Finance 1990, 5). Thus, in many ways, even after independence, institutions that were put in place by the British for colonizing Indians were partially transformed but never totally repudiated.

Despite the concrete transfer of power from British to Indian hands on August 15, 1947, important interpretive and institutional continuities existed in the imagining and the governance of independent India. While the moment of Indian independence was a juridical empowerment of India as a state in the international system, it did not necessarily suggest a structural break with colonial history. The social imaginary—the field of social meanings and powers—productive of independent India had a longer and less than totally revolutionary history.

What then were the social meanings that facilitated Indian independence but also constrained it from a total repudiation of its

colonial legacy? An investigation of the social imaginary productive of the nationalist movement and an independent India helps us answer this question. It entails analyzing the social claims articulated by Indian nationalists as they struggled to differentiate themselves from the British.

IMAGINING AN INDEPENDENT INDIA

The Indian nationalist movement underwent many changes in its long-drawn-out struggle against the British. It had different leaders and went through many distinct phases. I do not wish to get into the historical nuances, but I do intend to draw attention to some of the interpretive boundaries within which it was waged.

At the center was a concern over the progressive impoverishment of India under British rule. The nationalist movement, in highlighting this, advanced some critical claims about the politically appropriate relationships between the nation, the economy, and the state. I wish to confine my attention to some of those relationships and the ways in which they alert us to two powerful modes of differentiating the self within the social imaginary of Indian nationalism.

Searching for the reasons behind India's growing impoverishment, nationalist economists held the British state directly responsible (Dutt 1901, 1903; Naoroji 1901; Dasgupta 1993). While the British were not the first or the only conquerors of India, these economists argued that British rule exhibited a substantial difference from the rule of earlier conquerors and of other states in the international system. They argued that the British state did not concern itself with enriching the Indian nation economically. R. C. Dutt[10] argued that the British state in India not only did not increase the productive powers of its Indian nationals but also benefited at their expense (1901, xxv). This was in sharp contrast to existing standards of other states—such as England, Germany, the United States, or France—that identified with their nations, increased their productive powers, and benefited along with them.

One could, however, have argued that while the British state's relationship with the Indian nation did not reflect prevailing standards, such an indifferent or exploitative relationship (of the state to the nation) was by no means new within Indian history. The British were not the first rulers or even the worst in terms of establishing an exploitative relationship between the state and the nation. So why,

one could ask, make a big deal about this? After all, the British had not come to India to benefit the Indians.

Nationalist economists foreclosed that discursive escape by establishing another strong historical difference in the state-nation relationship. They argued that the British state differed from other earlier conquerors in not being completely aligned with the nation in terms of its economic practices. The British state did not spend the tax revenues it collected from the Indian nation within the nation itself, but instead transferred and spent them in other places. Dutt, in a famous passage, likened the appropriate fiscal relationship between the state and the nation to that between the sun and the "moisture of the earth." The moisture that is "sucked up" by the sun should always be "returned to the earth as fertilizing rain" (1901, xxv–xxvi).

For the nationalist economists, British exploitation lay not only in the amount of taxation—which did not necessarily differentiate the British from previous rulers—but in its space of circulation. The British did not recirculate the wealth they extracted within the territorial space of the Indian nation. They scorched this territorial space, which was bad enough, to fertilize other lands, which was worse. In draining the Indian nation of its "moisture" but not returning it as "fertilizing rain," the British were directly responsible for the growing poverty of the Indian nation. This one-way relationship between the state and the nation established the British as different from other rulers.

Notwithstanding disagreements about the significance and extent of such a drain,[11] the British state's relationship with the Indian nation and economy came to be articulated as considerably different, in terms of both contemporary and historical standards, from the relationships among other states. Such claims—that the British were unconcerned about the nation and that they were draining or bleeding the Indian nation to enrich other lands—proved to be extremely powerful in fueling the nationalist movement (Dasgupta 1993; Chandra 1966).

This is the beginning of a distinction—between the Self and the Other—that dominates the social imaginary of Indian nationalism. Such a Self-Other relationship distinguished the colonizer, the exploiter, the foreigner not by race or color or degree of exploitative taxation, but by its location outside the territorial boundaries of the

nation. The postcolonial Self thus defined itself against a territorially outside Other. The territorial outsider was the colonizer, the
exploiter to be vigorously resisted. But this was not the only Other.

While critical of the draining of Indian wealth by the British
state, the nationalists did not—in this phase—use the outsider
status of the British state to argue for an Indian state that would
be completely separate. Many analysts asserted that British colonial exploitation was incompatible with true Britishness and saw it
as the result of "unBritish rule" (Naoroji 1901). In other words,
for the nationalists, there was nothing inherently problematic with
the Britishness or the Westernness of the colonial regime. The
Britishness of the colonial apparatus did not mark it as a complete and obvious outsider. The nationalists wanted—initially at
least—to fit the Indian nation more securely into the British Empire,
without disarticulating it from British governance in any way. Dutt
observed, "In India, the people honestly desire a longer connection
with the British; not through sentimental loyalty, but . . . through
a sense of self-interest." That "self-interest" led them to believe
that they had "much to gain by being in close touch with the West"
(1901, xxviii).

How was it possible, one could ask, that the same nationalists
who claimed that the British were exploiting the Indian nation were
also those arguing for a longer connection with them? The answer
to that question touches on an important aspect of the nationalist
social imaginary and the other boundary against which the Indian
nationalists defined themselves and India: premodern India.

In order to understand this, one must understand the social meanings productive of the nationalist leaders. Indian nationalists were
the hybrid product of India's encounter with the British (Habib
1988, 55 56). They were produced and circulated in the border
trade between India and Britain. While they held the British responsible for India's material impoverishment—differentiating it from
earlier regimes—they also felt a great indebtedness to Britain (and
the West) for its contribution of "modernity." As modern products
themselves, they identified strongly with the British and saw an aspect of their own Self in the West. Dutt is quite explicit in admiring
the British for, among other things, providing a "strong and effica-
cious" administration and introducing "modern thought" to an
"ancient and civilized nation" (1901, xxi).

The encounter with Britain and the West, while oppressive in many ways, was read by the nationalists as emancipatory in other ways. There was a lot to be learned from the modern West such that a complete break with it, a total turning inward, was never a desirable option. In the nationalist social imaginary, admiration for the achievements of the modern West—its scientific and technical progress, its legal structure, its material power—was widely prevalent. As Nehru debated with Gandhi, "You have stated somewhere that India has nothing to learn from the West. . . . I entirely disagree with this viewpoint and I neither think the so-called Rama Raj was very good in the past, and nor do I want it back. I think Western or rather industrial civilization is bound to conquer India."[12] This strong identification with the West and with its industrial civilization was premised on a definition of the modern Indian Self against an internal, premodern India that had lost its way and needed to be brought back into the mainstream of a modern international system (Nehru 1961, 286). This meant overcoming many "lacks" in India and "developing" it into a modern nation-state (Chatterjee 1986; Seth 1995).

The nationalists saw themselves as modern and capable of engaging themselves in that task of transforming and developing premodern India into a modern one (Nehru 1961, 270). What was needed was a way of doing it that did not subordinate India once again to an external colonialism. Over the course of the nationalist struggle, the dominant understanding of the nation and national identity was framed by this fight against the twin dangers of a colonial West and a premodern India.[13] This imagining of an independent India—independent of the outside exploiter, intimate with Western modernity, resisting colonialism but also determined to resist premodernity—dominated the nationalists who finally achieved power on August 15, 1947. Postcoloniality came to imply neither a revolution nor a total break from the colonizer, but a carefully mediated separation that would erase an economically exploitative relationship without erasing the benefits of modernity that it had brought.

THE POSTCOLONIAL SELF

External colonialism and *internal premodernity* were thus the defining boundaries of the nationalist imagining of India. What then marks the postcolonial social identity is its continuity with and discontinuity from both the Western colonizer and the premodern Indian. This produces in the postcolonial Self a perpetual tension in reproducing itself through two contrasting modes of differentiation: one where it separates itself from its colonizer by emphasizing its difference with it and another where it separates itself from its premodern Self by identifying with the colonizer. I follow postcolonial theorists in conceptualizing this ambivalence in terms of the post-colonial's mimicry of and resistance to the colonizer (Chatterjee 1986; Prakash 1992; Bhabha 1994).

Colonization, it has been argued, is "a form of self-inscription onto the lives of a people who are conceived of as an extension of the landscape" (Spurr 1993, 7). Postcoloniality, on that reading, can be understood as a "writing back" of the hitherto colonial subjects. This writing back, to the extent that it is addressed to the colonizer, is in and through the institutions and regimes of the colonizer. It utilizes the language, the resources, the institutions, the norms, and the tools of the colonizer. In this sense, it is already at a distance from the native who does not have access to or is not empowered and differentiated through this colonial apparatus. But the postcolonial Self also utilizes these institutions to emphasize a difference from the colonizer: a different experience, a different message, a difference that is not quite the same performance as the colonizer's. In Homi Bhabha's evocative characterization, it is a difference that is "not white/not quite." The historical production of the colonial subject through the colonizer's regime marks the moment of mimicry, of imitation, and thus of the postcolonial's complicity in the continued reproduction of an oppressive, colonizing apparatus; however, the utilization of the same regime to undermine it, to assert its differ-ence, marks the moment of repugnance, repudiation, and resistance. The postcolonial identity is thus characterized by a strongly ambiva-lent identity-logic: a strong articulation of repugnance and a repu-diation of the colonizer, but also its mimicry.

The Indian nationalists, as the historical products of a post-colonial social imaginary, were marked with a similar ambivalence. They occupied and patrolled the borders between the majority of India's (premodern) nationals and the (colonizing) Westerners, but they themselves belonged wholly to neither space. They claimed their authority by mediating the relationship between the national and the Westerner—the insider and the outsider—without completely identifying themselves with one or the other. To the premodern Indian they presented themselves and re-presented the benefits of modernity. They were thus fellow Indians who had "transcended" their parochial, provincial, premodern limitations to enjoy the fruits of modernity—fruits that they now wished their premodern and parochial compatriots to enjoy. But since, historically, modernity had come in from the outside and hand in hand with colonization, it was important to mediate this relationship such that the colonizing outsider was kept out even as the premodern was transformed/developed inside into the fully modern.

To the outsider, the Westerner, the postcolonials acted as the civilizationally rich and ancient face of India. They cited ancient scripture and English verse to assert a different worldview on Afro-Asian relations and on the international system. They secured the national and the nation's space by keeping the Westerner at bay. But they also repudiated the existing, historically given nationness in the name of making it modern. Verily, they policed the border between the colonizer and the colonized, the Westerner and the Indian, the insider and the outsider, but in policing these borders they also reproduced themselves and their social powers. Jawaharlal Nehru, India's first prime minister, was the material and intellectual embodiment of this nationalist, postcolonial self.

What this implies for our understanding of state action is that a postcolonial social space functions through a distinctive identity-logic that operates by balancing a continuous mimicry of the colonizing outsider with a repudiation expressed as a difference from the colonizer. Based on this identity-logic, the internal tensions aroused by a postcolonial state's strategies of mimicry are erased by a strong repudiation that asserts its difference. The social identity of the postcolonial was reproduced by a matching of mimicry with mockery.

THE MATERIALIZATION OF SELF-RELIANCE

India, as an imagined community, is a postcolonial space with all its attendant ambivalence toward the outsider: the colonizing but modern West. Those who are empowered by this space are the modern nationals, the only complete citizens of India. The social institutions as well as the practices constitutive of this modern national community are marked by this ambivalence that secured India from its twin dangers: colonialism from outside and premodernity from inside.

Self-reliance, as an economic practice, was the historical manifestation of this ambivalence. As an economic policy, self-reliance was invested with at least three distinct sediments of social meanings. It was the crystallization of processes of nationalization, modernization, and endogenization.

Nationalization involved the renewed production of the Indian self in historically changed circumstances. It involved, among other things, a government-aided effort to produce a distinctive socio-economic space that could be called the national economy. Such a task acquired critical significance for the political leadership if we remember that independence from the British was accompanied by a partition of the subcontinent into India and Pakistan.[14] This was followed very soon by a consolidation of various small kingdoms into the Indian Union.[15] Given the political separation and consolidation of various territories through this process, political leadership was needed to suture a space of historically different economic regions into one coherently articulated and distinct economy.[16] But the production of a national economy meant not just the geographic or economic integration of different territories but also the "emotional" production of a recognizably Indian economy. The political leadership saw one important sign of national unity in the reduction of strong regional and social disparities. Balanced economic growth through planning thus constituted an important way of knitting the nation together emotionally.[17]

Modernization entailed a transformation of the national economic space in order to overcome its premodern features. The Indian National Congress—the party that formally came to power—had constituted a National Planning Committee for modernizing the economy long before the achievement of formal independence. The major industrialists of the nation had produced their own Bombay Plan. Indian leftists and the Gandhians had their plans, too (see Chakravarty 1987, 7). In spite of the various differences, the Nehruvian Congress, the industrialists, and the leftists were united against the Gandhians by their shared commitment to modernization. The Gandhians had a vision of India that was considerably nonmodern in its implications and unapologetically so (Chakravarty 1987, 8). In the end, the economic project the state ended up pursuing was the modernizing elite's vision of India (Chatterjee 1993; Seth 1995; Byres 1995; Chakravarty 1987).

Modernization was the moment of mimicry. It necessitated catching up with a pattern of development that was derived from outside India.[18] The Soviet experience of rapid industrial transformation had heavily influenced some segments of the modernizing elite.[19] Others had a more capitalist, Western vision. But within the elite, the idea of the government modernizing the economic space through a coordinated set of practices united them all (except the Gandhians) (see also Singh 1969, 353–54).

The stress on nationalization and modernization also led the government to endogenize or internalize many traditionally external constraints on its actions. The need for external resources—especially foreign exchange—was one such extremely important constraint to be overcome. While the political leadership did not rule out any dependence on foreign aid, it constantly emphasized that this would be only a short-term feature and that it would not be allowed to interfere with the course of internal economic policy.[20]

Resource constraints were also met by a strong mobilization of domestic savings from the national community for investment in large public sector projects. Further, given the scarcity of external and internal resources, the government strongly controlled the specific nature of industrialization followed by the private sector. This meant, for instance, a strict control on investments and economic activities that were directed toward the production of luxury goods—as defined by the government. Such investments were seen as socially wasteful. An additional aspect of endogenization was the government's effort to minimize India's reliance on the imports of food.[21]

Endogenization thus meant a deliberate effort at internalizing as many critical external constraints as possible. It was explicitly aimed at reducing the national economy's dependence on external Others. But even as India caught up with the industrializing countries, even as it benefited from their pattern of development, it did not "wish" to "copy" such "foreign models" (Nehru 1964, 405). Why would it not want to do that? What is it that would be lost by doing so? On the political leadership's understanding, India would not do that because its own individuality should be retained. In other words, it would catch up with the modern West, but it would not copy it. It would benefit from the West, but it would not repeat the same performance because doing so would mean a loss of its own history, traditions, and individuality. Endogenization, then, constituted the moment of repudiation.

The economic policy of self-reliance was thus multiply invested in terms of social meanings. It condensed the identity-logic of the postcolonial space into three different layers of social meanings. Such interpretive investments only intensified under the leaderships that followed Nehru.[22] While these layers were given different emphases under leaders such as Indira Gandhi, the overall meanings of self-reliance were not altered significantly until the beginning of economic restructuring in 1991.

The political leadership implemented the social meanings condensed in self-reliance by creating and empowering institutions such as the Planning Commission to nationalize, modernize, and endogenize the economy. The most significant of the Planning Commission's practices were the regular Five Year Plans that sketched and implemented specific nationally negotiated schemes for transforming the economy (Planning Commission 1956, 6). Planning made the government the main agency for economic activities (18). It allowed the government to increase its own control over the space of the economy. It facilitated an endogenization of significant aspects of external stimuli needed for economic growth (Bose and Mukherjee 1985, 75). It allowed the government to achieve not just an immediate increase in the supply of goods produced within the national economy but also a longer-term increase in the internal capacity to generate and sustain economic expansion. The social meanings and practices of self-reliance thus produced and reproduced a postcolonial nation—a postcolonial India. Within this postcolonial India, there was a distinctive distribution of social relations and powers.

The socioeconomic space was demarcated into various public, private, and joint sectors, redistributing the social powers of production—who was empowered to produce what, where, and in what quantities—asymmetrically between the government and private economic actors. The government reserved for itself the commanding heights of the economy and shared a joint responsibility with the private sector in other areas. The government and its bureaucrats were thus the main economic actors within the Indian economic space. Other, more conventional, economic actors such as industrialists had to be periodically empowered by the government—through the granting of licenses and permits—to function within specific spheres. The rest of the people, however, were the intended beneficiaries (and thus the objects) of this process that concentrated economic agency primarily in the political leadership, the government bureaucrats, and the Indian industrialists.

Economic liberalization appears in this postcolonial space then as a change in the policy of self-reliance. But, given the social imaginary constitutive of meanings within this space, any movement away from self-reliance, though intended as only a change in economic strategy, is interpellated very differently by the postcolonials. The social imaginary transforms a seemingly technical or pragmatic change in strategy to a dangerous threat to national identity. How so? I offer an answer in the next section through a close reading of a reformer's text.

THE POLITICS OF LIBERALIZATION

Pranab Mukherjee was a powerful and senior member of the Congress Party and also an active advocate of economic reforms during the Congress regime (1991–1996). He presided over critical ministries—including finance, commerce, and external affairs—in the cabinets of Indira Gandhi, Rajiv Gandhi, and P. V. Narasimha Rao. In a speech to Indian diplomats in early 1996, he outlined the government's understandings of the economic reforms it had initiated.[23]

Mukherjee begins with the claim that there is a direct relationship between the growth rate of the economy and its requirements of specific levels of investment.[24] This implies that if domestic savings (savings inside the national economic space) happened to be less than the level of investment required to finance a specifically targeted growth rate, the difference could be met through external resources. But external resources (the resources of the Other) presented both a threat and an opportunity to the government.

In expanding on the threat and opportunity posed by external resources, Mukherjee argues that India had managed—through heavy borrowing—to break the economic stagnation it experienced from 1960 to 1980.[25] This allowed it to achieve higher growth rates in the VI and VII Five Year Plan periods but also contributed directly to the 1991 economic crisis.[26] In linking an economic policy that relied on external resources to a subsequent economic crisis, Mukherjee acknowledges the dangers implicit in the Self's reliance on the Other. The external world (the Other) is recognized as a potential threat to the national Self—as it has consistently been in the arguments of the nation-claimers.

But Mukherjee also delimits the areas within which the threat from the Other can be managed. He concretizes this by specifying the trade-offs involved between growth rates and the levels of investment needed. He argues that if the government wanted a sustained growth rate of 5.5 percent per annum, it only needed a level of investment equivalent to 22 to 23 percent of the country's gross domestic product (GDP).[27] Given that existing domestic savings were at 21.6 percent of GDP, the government would need, Mukherjee claims, resources of approximately 1.6 percent of GDP annually. This, he believes, could be met through external borrowing and constituted "a manageable level of reliance" on the outside world. Moreover, under such conditions, the government had no need to rely on any additional foreign (direct) investment. That is, if there was a need for only a small portion (1.6 percent of GDP) of the Other's resources, the Self could borrow the resources from the Other but need not invite it into the national economic space.

What prevented the government from being comfortable with such rates of growth, however, was the danger that would arise not from outside the country but from within the nation. On the government's understanding, the critical issue was not just its capacity to manage an external threat—based on a specific level of external borrowings and a targeted internal rate of growth that it was comfortable with—but its capacity to manage an internal threat under such conditions of low growth. Mukherjee points out that with a targeted rate of growth of 5.5 percent, the "existing backlog of unemployment" would not be addressed even by the year 2010. He wonders, even if the government was willing to wait that long, would "our people . . . wait so long?" In other words, the government, as the manager of the economy, recognizes not just a threat from an excessive reliance on outside resources but also a threat that might emerge—with insufficient rates of growth—from within the nation.[28] That is, while the situation was manageable in terms of the danger posed by the external Other, it was not so in terms of the dangers posed by the Self to itself.

Tackling this threat, Mukherjee asserts, involves raising the targeted rates of growth. He points out that raising the targeted growth rate to 7 percent per annum would allow the government to solve the unemployment problem by 2002–3. But this would require levels of investment equivalent to 28 to 29.5 percent of GDP each year and—with existing levels of domestic savings—would entail external resource flows of 7 to 8.5 percent. In Mukherjee's opinion, such a level of dependence on external borrowing constituted an "unmanageable" level of foreign borrowing that would only drive India into a "debt trap" and make economic growth unsustainable in the long run (Mukherjee 1996, 7–9). Too much borrowing from the Other was thus not only unmanageable but also destructive of the Self's long-term growth. But the threat from the Self itself left it with no option but to aim for higher growth rates. In this context, Mukherjee observes: "This is where foreign investment becomes critical. It enables us to target higher growth rates without running into the dangers posed by external indebtedness" (7–9).

So the government invites foreign investment because it constitutes a manageable way to tackle the dual dangers of too much reliance on external borrowings and too low a rate of growth inside. The Other is invited into the national economic space because it appears—to the reformers—to be the most manageable way of combating the twin dangers from the Self and the Other. A refusal to rely at all on the Other or too little a reliance on the Other's resources meant unsatisfactory rates of growth within the national economy and hence a great danger from within the Self itself. Too much borrowing of the Other's resources meant a danger of indebtedness and the threat of an unsustainable growth path. The only way out was to invite the Other in to facilitate higher levels of investment, increase the rates of economic growth, and contain the danger from within.

But the Other, on the reformers' understanding, had some additional attractions (Mukherjee 1996, 7–9). It possessed superior technology that could force a critical part of the national economy—domestic industry—to become more efficient. In doing this it might also make it possible for the Self to utilize its capital more efficiently and thus obviate the need for a greater dependence on the Other (in the long run).

It needs to be noted that this positive articulation of the Other is enabled by a careful separation of the effects of foreign investments on domestic industry from their effects on the country as a whole (which would benefit from the effects of such an efficiency on the part of domestic industry). In doing this, Mukherjee delimits the Other as a threat only to inefficient industry and portrays it as a boon to the country as a whole. In thus rearticulating the threat posed by external resources, Mukherjee explicitly acknowledges and takes up the potential threats that foreign investment—as the Other—might pose to the country (the Self) (1996, 7–9). But the discursive strategy for dealing with that threat remains much the same. In acknowledging the competition inherent in both foreign and domestic industry fighting over the same pool of domestic investable funds, Mukherjee divorces domestic industry from a distinctive "we" (the Self identified as the "savers" and the "nation"). He then links the foreign and the domestic together as a set of entrepreneurs (and thus as risk-taking groups different from the nation) and reads their conflict over investable funds as a limited, internal conflict among risk-taking entrepreneurs.

The potential appeal that domestic entrepreneurs could make here on the basis of their shared Indian identity is muted by defining them primarily as entrepreneurs struggling against Other entrepreneurs, rather than as Indians struggling against the competition of non-Indian foreigners. Since "we" are not part of this conflict but are on the outside, the outcome of the conflict can only be beneficial to those of us who are non-entrepreneurs and "savers." "We"—as the Self sans inefficient industrialists—would gain from a productive and efficient use of "our" resources.

Mukherjee deals with the additional fears of the Other more explicitly. Wouldn't foreign companies—the Other invited inside— threaten the economic sovereignty of the Indian nation? Once inside our economic space, wouldn't these powerful Others bring the Self under their control? How was the government so confident that it could manage multinational corporations? On these issues, Mukherjee claims that the belief that "the entire industrial economy of the country would pass into the hands of foreigners" is a "misplaced fear." It arises because of an inability to understand "the magnitudes involved and the nature of the Indian economy." Moreover, India was not a "banana republic" that could be "swamped by foreign inflows," nor were its business people so "incompetent" that they could not "compete effectively with multinationals." It was, Mukherjee notes, "the very complexity of our economy" that was "sufficient guarantee of this belief." To assume otherwise "would be an insult and a denigration of our own abilities and self-respect" (1996, 7–9).

Mukherjee effects some notable discursive moves in this passage. First of all, he recuperates for the national Self those very firms that he had divorced from "our" country a few passages earlier. These firms are now "our" firms and these entrepreneurs are "our" entrepreneurs in whose ability to compete "we" have a lot of faith. Further, Mukherjee turns around the whole set of fears about the foreign as misplaced signs that do not do justice to what India (the Self) is and what our abilities (the Self's abilities) are. India is not a banana republic, he asserts. That is, we cannot easily be bought by outsiders (1996, 7–9).

Moreover, the space of the inside—the economy and its resources—was so vast and complex that it could not easily be overwhelmed by the foreign. Given "our" abilities and the size and complexity of "our" economy, Mukherjee claims, there is little need to fear the Other. There is so little need that such a fear or lack of faith can only be taken as an offense or as a reflection on the nature of the national Self. No other response, Mukherjee seems to imply, would be appropriate.[29]

The political reformers' support of economic restructuring seems then to emerge from specific claims about the dual threats (from the Self and the Other) that the government faces as well as its relative capacities to manage them. On this set of claims, India's political and economic managers face a rising set of economic demands from within the nation that can be met only by higher rates of economic growth than the ones enjoyed (or suffered) so far. Higher growth rates require higher levels of investment in the national economic space, and this creates a need for the resources of the Other. Given the option of either borrowing the Other's resources or inviting the Other into the national economic space, the government perceives the latter as the more manageable threat. How are the reformers sure that, once inside, the Other will not dominate the Self? The confidence of the reformers is based on certain claims about what the national Self and its capacities are (vast, complex, competent) and what they are not ("not a banana republic") at this stage. Part of the confidence in managing foreign investment comes then from claims about the national Self and the national economic space. Another part is based on the understanding that the danger posed by the Other predominantly threatens a part that can be divorced from the Self—inefficient industry. Such a divorce, in fact, is seen as only strengthening the Self.

Rereading the script of Indian economic liberalization from the perspective of the policy makers reveals how the reformers are—in advancing social claims about the positive effects of inviting the Other into the national economic space—actually rearticulating the dominant narrative of the national, postcolonial Self. Within the social imaginary productive of postcolonial India, the Other was doubly marked as territorially outside the national economic space and as colonial. The outsider—the Other—is now being invited inside the national economic space and is being coded not as colonial (and hence exploitative and dominating of the Self) but as beneficial to the Self. To the extent that the social imaginary has conventionally reproduced India as a postcolonial space—based on a different understanding of Self-Other relations—existing channels of social communication cannot relay these rearticulations very well or are interpreted in ways that make sense within the social imaginary, i.e., as a blatant invitation to the Other to come into the national economic space—the inside—and exploit and dominate the Self. The result is the consistent interpretation of the reformers as mortgaging India's economic sovereignty and the claim that the ruling party lacks shame and is following the dictates of colonial forces.

UNDERSTANDING INDIAN ECONOMIC LIBERALIZATION

If we take the economic reformers' social claims seriously, economic liberalization is an attempt to increase the pace of modernization in order to ward off internal dangers from economic stagnation. Given the constraints on domestic resources, foreign direct investment is being invited to play a critical role in this accelerated process of modernization. This is an explanation that would be conventionally offered by the mainstream economists also.

Narrowly reading the reasons offered by Mukherjee as evidence of economic rationality on the part of the Indian government (however belated), most rationalist explanations in international relations would focus on seeing how this "economically rational" policy was pushed through against a variety of countervailing forces. They would focus on who supported this policy, who opposed it, how a crisis made this choice inevitable, and how, finally, one policy prevailed over another. Such an explanatory strategy would entail bracketing a whole area of analysis as the domain of economic logic and then explaining how this logic was successful within the governing party. Against such explanations, a historical-materialist explanation would see Mukherjee's reasons as essentially an ideological cover-up for some real interests working behind the scene. These could be the domestic bourgeoisie, the transnational bourgeoisie, or fractions thereof. The rationalists would thus focus primarily on the economic logic in Mukherjee's analysis; the historical-materialists would discount his economic reasoning altogether. I would argue that both miss the point.

What is most interesting about Mukherjee's speech is that economic reason, power, and politics are all woven together in some very intricate ways. As I have illustrated through my reading, his reasoning is not just economic but also deeply political. The identities, and derivatively the interests, of different groups are invoked and empowered or disempowered through very specific articulations.

Next I want to illustrate how a critical constructivist analysis of Indian economic restructuring offers us some important answers that rationalists and historical-materialists have no way of accessing. More specifically, I claim that my critical constructivist reading resolves some distinct questions about the nature of Indian economic liberalization that are difficult for rationalists and historical-materialists to answer.

POSTCOLONIAL SOVEREIGNTY AND STRATEGY

Indian economic space, as I illustrated earlier, is a postcolonial space. From the perspective of a postcolonial social imaginary with its attendant identity-logic, modernization—as a mimicry of the West—must always be matched by a repudiation of the West. That which is being imitated must also be mocked and disclaimed. It is the balance between mimicking and rejection that reproduces the postcolonial identity. What economic liberalization does in turning away from self-reliance, especially the focus on endogenization, is to upset an earlier balance between modernization as mimicry, and endogenization and nationalization as repudiation. Under earlier economic regimes, the government's policy of self-reliance—condensing nationalization, modernization, and endogenization—allowed the stable reproduction of a postcolonial identity by matching the imitative moment of modernization with the repudiation inherent in nationalization and endogenization.[30] But economic liberalization—as a change in economic strategy that reduces the role of the government within domestic economic space and invites the Other in—is a dilution or oftentimes a reversal of the nationalizing and endogenizing aspects of self-reliance. This means that at the same time as there is a heightened mimicking of the modern West there is no contrasting effort by the government at repudiating it. Such an absence of the practices of repudiation interrupts the hitherto continuous relay of social meanings, powers, and identities productive of postcolonial India.

An interruption in such relays implies that the reformers have no persuasive answers to the postcolonial questions: If we are imitating the modernity of the West, if we are constantly trying to catch up with our erstwhile colonizer, in what sense are we different? How are we postcolonial if we are always trying to be like our historical colonizer? If there is no difference between us and them, between the modern Indian Self and the modern Western Other, are we not still a colony? Has colonization not determined us so completely that we are incapable of even developing differently? At what site or through what social practices is our difference, our independence, our postcoloniality, our presence after colonialism, our "not white/not quite" identity being performed?

The failure to offer convincing answers to these questions destabilizes the relay of social meanings, powers, and identities that are productive of the postcolonial agency of the government. This is because, given the absence of a repudiation of the modern West, there is little to differentiate the colonized government (which mimics the modern West on the orders, the dictates, of the colonial West) from the ostensibly independent, postcolonial government (which mimics the West of its own volition but has no site or social practices to perform its difference). It is the gap between an increasing mimicry and a decreasing mockery that results in a credibility problem for the reforming regime and explains the proliferation of charges of "comprador-ness" hurled at the restructuring government. It is for these reasons that economic liberalization manifests itself within India not as a technical change in economic policy but as a crisis of national identity. It becomes therefore the site not of a debate on the efficiency of different economic policies, of different methods, or of different interests alone, but the site of a test for the postcolonial Self, for the postcoloniality of the Indian nation.

This explanation, however, leads to another question: if the postcolonial social imaginary is so powerful, how was economic liberalization undertaken at all and then carried on for so long? I would argue that what facilitated economic restructuring within a postcolonial polity was a very creative act of political agency. This creativity lay in the deliberate rearticulation of Indianness from a predominantly territorial conception to an increasingly deterritorialized one. The social meanings of Indianness have been gradually freed—juridically—from a territorial anchoring. In the last two decades, a new social identity has been socially and legally empowered within Indian politics and through the Indian government's policies. This new social identity is that of the diasporic or nonresident Indian (NRI).

The NRIs, at one level, can be seen as the new postcolonials. The NRIs are neither Self nor Other, but both Self and Other. They inhabit the spaces of the West and of India. As residents of the West, NRIs are very intimate with modernity. But as persons of Indian origin (it doesn't really matter how many centuries ago they originated), NRIs are also coded as successfully reproducing Indianness in alien spaces and of forever desiring to return home. The difficult problem of getting the modern West in without losing premodern India has been partially resolved through the bodies of the NRIs. The NRIs provide a safe, secure, and reassuring conduit for foreignness in the form of capital, skills, technology, and investment. The economic success and cultural obduracy of NRIs in the modern West is read as proof of India's potential success in dealing with Western forces. When Microsoft, Oracle, and IBM come into the Indian space, the faces they present to India are mostly those of expatriate Indians coming home. The NRI is now the "true" postcolonial, reassuring the West and reassuring to the resident Indians. If economic liberalization has been possible in India, it is primarily because of and through the ambiguous but increasingly powerful and postcolonial identities of the NRI.

In analyzing the politics of economic liberalization in India, I began by taking seriously the social claims of various proponents and opponents of these practices. I showed how they all shared and were empowered by a common discourse of the nation that dominated any attempt to deal with the issues on the basis of economic reason alone. Reconstructing the historically institutional-ized meanings of the nation, I argued that these were productive of a postcolonial Indian identity that is powerfully constitutive of national interests and state practices in domestic and international politics. Understanding the politics of the global in India thus ne-cessitates understanding the varied negotiations of its postcolonial identity.

4

Globalization in the United States

"Everything in America hinges on success, and we don't have an awful lot of time for losers," he [Michael A. Ledeen] said by way of explaining the American mind. ". . . If people get in the way, we say, 'Get outta my way.' Most Americans have always been in a great hurry."

COURTLAND MILLOY, WASHINGTON POST

"There was one Iraqi soldier, and 25 women and children," he said, "I didn't take the shot." But more than once, Sergeant Schrumpf said, he faced a different choice: one Iraqi soldier standing among two or three civilians. He recalled one such incident, in which he and other men in his unit opened fire. He recalled watching one of the women standing near the Iraqi soldier go down. "I'm sorry," the sergeant said. "But the chick was in the way."

DEXTER FILKINS, NEW YORK TIMES

The National Security Strategy doctrine of the Bush administration received much attention for its ostensibly dramatic difference from established U.S. security strategy (Gaddis 2002). Commentators argued over the novelty of its formulations, especially its focus on preemptive strikes and its straightforward assertion of a desire to prevent any other state from challenging the power of the United States in the international system. John Lewis Gaddis (2002) argued that this "could be . . . the most important reformulation of U.S. grand strategy in over a century." Strong assertions of a dramatic change notwithstanding, a common claim united both the old and new grand strategies: the government of the United States had a unique responsibility to lead the rest of the world.

Claiming that freedom was a universal value, the Bush administration's National Security Strategy identified not only the various threats faced by freedom but also the unique opportunity for freedom to finally prevail over all of these threats. Most intriguing was that it effortlessly placed the burden of defending this universal value on the United States. Though different in strategy and in tone, the Clinton administration's National Security Strategy, issued in 1999, articulated a similar claim, asserting that the United States was "called upon to lead."

What makes such a claim to leadership puzzling from my perspective is the explicit relationship it posits to the global community. The United States sees itself as called on to lead the world, but who exactly among the different groups in the world is calling the United States to do so? Where are these voices, which the United States claims to be hearing, coming from? If, as the Bush National Security Strategy educates us, "freedom" is the "birthright of every person," in "every civilization," and that "humanity" finally has the "opportunity" to advance "freedom's triumph," how and when did the government of the United States, and not any of the nearly two hundred other governments or multiple other nonstate organizations, get selected for this "great mission"?

The claim to global leadership is quite pervasive, almost commonsensical, in the dominant U.S. discourses about global issues. Such a claim seems to resonate well not only with U.S. government agencies[1] but also with business groups,[2] organized labor,[3] organizations such as the Project for a New American Century,[4] and even NGOs.[5] But I want to focus less on the claim to global leadership than on the implicit relationship to the rest of the world that is posited here. What is the politics that links "global" to "leadership" in U.S. social claims about "global leadership"?

The answer, to foreshadow much of the argument that follows, is that the politics of this relationship to the others in the world is primarily a colonial one because, despite the crucial prominence of the idea of democracy in the U.S. imaginary, U.S. security and economic discourses hardly exhibit a dialogical or democratic relation to difference. Second, even though the call to lead is articulated as a responsibility placed on U.S. shoulders by others, a closer examination reveals not the voices of others but only those of the self. Global leadership, in the U.S. imaginary, is essentially a mandate that the American Self gives to itself. Others, to the extent that they count at all, are only projected and frequently pale reflections of the Self.

I will read closely some prominent accounts of U.S. identity and ideology to show how various colonizing practices are not fully teased out in some critical analyses of U.S. identity. I will then discuss what this means for the politics of the global in terms of dominant U.S. discourses.

GLOBAL LEADERSHIP AND THE LIBERAL U.S. IMAGINARY

To say that global leadership is an important self-conception within the U.S. imaginary is not necessarily a novel observation. Scholars, conventional (Walt 2002) as well as critical (Weldes 1999; Rupert 1995, 2000), have often referred to this claim in discussing U.S. economic and security policies. But the terms of their discussions have often bypassed or underexplored the colonial politics of such a claim. I will explore the analysis of two critical scholars—Jutta Weldes and Mark Rupert—who, in my view, come closest to a perceptive analysis of this aspect of U.S. identity but still don't go far enough.

Rupert (2000) offers a comprehensive reconstruction of the social meanings productive of the ideology of globalization. His work lays out, quite carefully, the changes in ideological and material structures that were constitutive of American hegemony initially and the project of liberal globalization subsequently. There is much that is noteworthy in Rupert's analysis, but, in terms of my argument here, his development of American hegemony as a combination, in a Gramscian fashion, of coercion and consent is especially relevant. Examining the common sense underlying the production of American hegemony and its rearticulation in the context of U.S. debates over globalization, Rupert identifies three sets of social groups that were crucial actors in this context: liberal proponents of globalization, opponents committed to democratic self-determination and transnational solidarities, and opponents wedded to an aggressive American exceptionalism and sectarianism.

Rupert's analysis reveals, quite insightfully, the power of liberal proponents to set the broad terms of the debate over globalization. Liberal proponents, priding themselves on the scientific nature of their economic knowledge, argued strongly for the benefits (greater efficiency, lower prices, more jobs, and higher incomes) that flowed from a subscription to the principles of comparative advantage, international competition, and economies of scale (2000, 49–64). But the other side of the liberal claim to reason was their frequent presentation of those who opposed globalization as unsophisticated in their technical expertise or irrational and dangerous. After laying out the terrain of this struggle, Rupert identifies an additional feature of liberal ideology: the U.S. claim to global leadership and responsibility. "As with NAFTA," Rupert observes, "the icing on the cake was the case for continuing global leadership and the danger that the liberal world order—with its imputed virtues of prosperity, peace, and democracy—might be supplanted by the 'law of the jungle' should the U.S. abdicate its global responsibilities" (64). Clearly, the proponents of liberal globalization articulated their case in a way that linked greater liberalization with economic reason, science, material benefits, and the continued U.S. leadership of a liberal world order. They implicitly portrayed their opponents as "dangerous" in lacking these features or as standing for their very opposites.

In explaining the politics of globalization in the United States, Rupert points out (2000, 62), quite correctly, that much of the debate was conducted on the "economistic terrain" of the liberal proponents. He argues that liberal categories had the "depoliticizing" effect of concealing the tensions between private property and democracy. They thereby transformed what should have been political arguments into seemingly technical issues at the same time as they rendered the arguments of the opponents "unintelligible" (58–59).

As an analysis of an ideological struggle, there is much that is valuable in this particular perspective. Rupert's argument clarifies, quite nicely, not only the social claims on the different sides but also the inequality of the material resources that were brought to bear on this issue by various groups. Notwithstanding these merits, Rupert does not take the analysis of the ideological terrain far enough. He does not explore, for instance, why these claims were so persuasive within the broader American imaginary. How did these articulations make sense to the public? Rupert's argument tells us that the outcome testified to the "hegemony of liberal doctrines," but it does not trace the discursive processes through which that hegemony was reproduced and secured.

From my perspective, Rupert's analysis itself offers an opening for answering these questions. The liberal construction of the opponents of globalization as irrational or dangerous is an important insight that can be explored further. Liberals, Rupert notes, present the first set of opponents, committed to transnational solidarities, as unscientific, while the second set of opponents, proclaiming American nationalism, are presented as xenophobic. The dominant ideological articulation marginalizes the cosmopolitan left on the basis of its lack of technical reason while the nationalistic right is marginalized on the basis of its lack of cosmopolitanism. The two lacks thus testify to and secure the border of a liberal Self that understands itself as rational, nationalist, and global. The liberal Self's claim to global leadership is the condensed form that is taken by this articulation of the rational, the national, and the global.

How is this seemingly contradictory articulation made persuasive? How can U.S. identity, to focus on one of the linkages here, come to be seen as simultaneously national and global? I argue that this is where Rupert's "icing on the cake" actually turns out to be central to the ideological struggle over globalization in the United States. Only a colonial relationship to the Others in the world can, as I will establish, articulate the rational and the national to the global in ways that are compelling within the liberal American imaginary.

If Rupert's analysis focused on the United States as it deals with the politics of the global economy, Weldes's work examines U.S. identity as it deals with issues of global security. Writing about U.S. foreign policy during the Cuban missile crisis, Weldes (1999) reconstructs, quite ably, how U.S. identity during this period was structured around the features of leadership, freedom, strength, and credibility. She argues that winning the Second World War and conceptions of U.S. uniqueness led to its claims of leadership.

How, one wonders, can winning and uniqueness lead to the burden of leadership? All nations imagine themselves as unique on some count or other (Anderson 1991). Arguably, that is the very condition of their nationness. And winning implicitly raises the question of the broader intersubjective context. What game is everyone playing? Did everyone or even many in the world share the United States' assumption that it had won the Second World War or even that it was something in which there were winners and losers? Answers to such questions require an engagement with the imaginations, understandings, and voices of other actors in the world. It is not apparent that such voices went into the U.S. conception of itself as a leader if the two dominant features of that understanding were winning and uniqueness. My point is not that the features Weldes points to are wrong as much as that they do not seem to link unproblematically to the assumption of a leadership role based on the demands of others. U.S. leadership, in Weldes's account, continues to remain a self-generated, self-endowed responsibility.

Weldes does, explicitly and insightfully, recognize the nonnecessary nature of articulations as she accounts for the linkage between leadership and the global (1999, 205). But she traces it to the linkage between U.S. identity and its claims about freedom. As she observes: "Central to the identity of the United States, and the major reason for its leadership role, was its articulation to freedom. . . . It was a society in which the virtue of freedom and its attendant institutions—in particular, representative or liberal democracy and a liberal market economy—had been more elaborately developed than in any other. . . . The United States thus could and should serve as a model or guide (a standard denotation of leader) to all those who aspired to a similar life" (205).

This is an interesting explanation in some ways. It offers an alternative account of how a claim to the burden of leadership can actually be a self-generated one provided it fulfills two conceptual requirements. The first is that there is a definition of leadership that makes sense even without the consent of those who are to be led, and the second is that the defining of what the presumed followers want is also in the hands of the leader. In other words, this conception of leadership, the burden of leadership, silences the voices of other actors in the world at two levels: it does not ask for their consent, and it presumes that it knows the truth of where they might want to go. The leader here, far from being only a model, appears to be a prophet, an unelected possessor of the correct Truth for everyone.

Weldes's analysis of the politics of U.S. identity in terms of this articulation revolves around three meaningful linkages. The first is that there is a conception of leadership that is not dependent on the explicit consent of others: the U.S. as a leader who is a model or guide. But the U.S. as a leader is a guide to what? It is a guide to "all those who aspired to a similar life" in this world. And the content of that similar life, rather than being up for negotiation and discussion, is once again decided without the involvement of those who are to be led through a third linkage. This is, as Weldes points out insightfully (206–7), that everyone else, everywhere in the world, had the same (the United States') conception of freedom (208).

Weldes (1999) reconstructs how the liberal imaginary makes these linkages appear meaningful and unproblematic, but she does not fully draw out from this liberal imaginary the colonial politics that political theorists such as Mehta (1999) have demonstrated so powerfully. At no stage in the production of this articulation—the definition of leadership, the understanding of what others want, the assumption that one knows where the others want to go—is there any effort at engaging the presumed followers in a dialogue. They are never brought into the picture but are always taken for granted.

Faced with a diverse world that it cannot credibly claim to know in all its diversity, the United States does not bother to ask if other actors might really want its leadership; it does not wonder if others really see it as a guide to a desirable conception of the good; it does not bother to ask if others have the same understanding of its achievements or uniqueness as it does or if they define universal ideals such as freedom in the same way. Neglecting all these multiple ways of relating dialogically to the others in the world, the liberal imaginary productive of the United States is systematically closed to the possibility of relating democratically to difference. Thus, if the U.S. identity is constituted through a liberal imaginary, it is also an imaginary that is simultaneously colonial in its orientation to others in the world. The colonial moment lies not in the claim of exceptionalism or uniqueness but in the belief that what is particular to the United States is actually universal, that what is local is actually global.[6] What implications does this have for how we understand the liberal American imaginary?

THE LIBERAL-COLONIAL IMAGINARY AND ITS ORIENTATION TO OTHERS

A liberal-colonial imaginary is one that is constituted dominantly by an assumption of the Self as the unproblematic and ultimate repository of Reason, Morality, and Power. Understood as a series of lacks from within this imaginary, Others appear as irrational, immoral, and weak beings in the world. The imaginary is constitutive of a rational, moral, and powerful humanism and a savage, barbarous, brutish Other. Liberation or liquidation then appears as the crucial strategy for relating to the human/brute differences.

Liquidation encounters the Other through the use of overwhelming power. It is the desire to control others coercively, even, if necessary, by annihilating them. "Exterminate all the brutes" or "Kill 'em all" are its rallying cries (Lindqvist 1996). In seeming contrast, liberation encounters the Other in order to save it, to salvage it from its brutish existence, by teaching it the correct Reason, Morality, and Power (Todorov 1999; Mehta 1999). "Dare to let them know" is its primary orientation.

The exterminatory strategy is facilitated by the claim that there are limits to reason and morality in engagements with the Other. And once those imagined limits have been reached, then Power remains the just (rational and moral) way of engaging the Other. If reason cannot reach them and morality fails to have an effect, then power can and must eliminate them. Of course, the understandings of the limits of reason, morality, and just strategies are generated from within the liberal-colonial imaginary itself—not from an engagement with the Other. The liberatory strategy emerges from the claim that the brute is an Other that, under the right conditions, is accessible to some forms of reason, morality, and even power. This is constitutive of many pedagogical moments in Self-Other encounters. What makes this less directly violent engagement possible is frequently the Other's relative lack of power. Within the liberal-colonial imaginary, it is self-evident that the brute's lack of power stems from its lack of access to reason and morality.

What brings these liberate and/or liquidate strategies together is the assumption of the exceptional nature of the Self that deploys them, which sees itself as uniquely complete in terms of reason, morality, and power. The moment of the Self here is also the moment of exceptionality and universality. In other words, the Self's moment of particularity is simultaneously its moment of universality. But the Other, in contrast, is always mired in its particularity. Thus, while it is acknowledged that the world is diverse, it is also known that no one is or can be as good, as rational, and as powerful as the Self.

It is quite understandable, within this imaginary, that Others might aspire toward or seek to achieve the completeness that is the unique property of the Self. But it is understood that few will manage to achieve that position of genuine equality. Implicit here is the belief that while the brutish Other can tend toward the rational-moral-powerful perfection of the Self, it is always inadequate in some ways. What is thus implicitly ruled out is any conception of the Other as an equally or more rational, equally or more powerful, and equally or more moral being: i.e., a conception of a Self that is equal or more but also different. It is this inability to comprehend a Self that is human but truly Other—i.e., an acknowledgment of radical diversity and difference—that makes the liberal imaginary's relation to Others in the world fundamentally colonial (Todorov 1999, 42).

It is this always already incomplete nature of Others in the world that makes it impossible, therefore, for the liberal-colonial imaginary to have a truly dialogical or democratic engagement with the rest of the world. Others are never really rational enough, moral enough, or powerful enough to be seen as one's equals. The only possible relation to the Other is the constant need to either fill such inadequacies or prevent them from threatening the Self. This means that the Self is constantly forced to either educate the Others or eliminate them.

The recognition of the colonial politics structuring the liberal-colonial imaginary makes it possible to constantly see the unifying threads behind what might appear to be discrete moments in the politics of the global. In the following section, I will demonstrate how a common thread of colonial politics unifies seemingly different invocations of the global in the United States.

COERCING THE OTHER

A survey of articles in some prominent Western journals and magazines reveals the reappearance of the idea of imperialism—a "new imperialism"—as a desirable form of global governance.[7] My initial response was incredulity at this nostalgia for a shameful past in world history. I couldn't help wondering what next: a new slavery, an enlightened patriarchy, or maybe a reluctant racism? It was particularly striking that these calls for a new imperialism were coming from fairly mainstream and influential sources such as *Foreign Affairs* and the *Financial Times*. But I quickly set aside my, no doubt naive, expectations of historical shame and decided to explore, a little more closely, the imaginative terrain that made such claims socially meaningful and ethically palatable.

Sebastian Mallaby's lead article in *Foreign Affairs* (2002), "The

Reluctant Imperialist," offers a useful entry into this discourse.[8] Mallaby's enthusiasm for the new imperialism springs from his concern about the "power vacuums" that arise in the international system when "chaotic states . . . provide profit and sanctuary to nihilist outlaws." After examining the various ways in which "disorder" in "poor countries" (also portrayed as "dysfunctional" and "failed states") threatens the "orderly ones" through the offering of sanctuary to "terrorists," the facilitation of "illegal drug supply," "criminal business," and "traffic in illegal workers," Mallaby argues that various "nonimperialist" responses such as "foreign aid" and "nation-building" have not proven "reliable" (3).

Given this unreliability of "nonimperialist" methods, Mallaby proposes a new "rich man's burden" for contemporary times, proclaiming, "The logic of neoimperialism is too compelling for the Bush administration to resist" (6). Mallaby does not think that this is necessarily an easy enterprise or one that the United States would take up willingly. "The United States," he asserts, "today will be an even more reluctant imperialist. But a new imperial moment has arrived, and by virtue of its power America is bound to play the leading role" (6).

U.S. reluctance, according to Mallaby, can be traced to two factors. The first is "the fear that empire is infeasible." In short, imperialism could be "expensive, difficult and potentially dangerous." The second is the incorrectly posed "stale choice between unilateralism and multilateralism." Mallaby dismisses the first objection by arguing that imperialism could be cost-effective. He constructs a more elaborate case against the second by claiming that "unilateral imperialism" is unlikely to work any better than the "muddled multilateral efforts" of the past (6).

So what would work? He suggests an "institutionalizing . . . [of a] mix of U.S. leadership and international legitimacy." Where does this "international legitimacy" come from? Is it based on careful political negotiations among different countries of the world, rich and poor? Not really. This "hybrid formula," Mallaby asserts, is already present in the World Bank and the IMF that "reflect American thinking and priorities yet are simultaneously multinational" (7).

How do we read these claims? It is clear from Mallaby's analysis that the reluctance that attaches to the imperialism he proposes is *not* the reluctance of *an ethical constraint*. We are not talking about the reluctant application of imperialism for the achievement of a larger, potentially justifiable, democratically agreed on, global good. In that sense, the relationship that appears here between the governors and the governed, the rich and the poor, the orderly and the disorderly is not one that could be expected in a global political community where different social actors have reciprocal obligations. The governed, the disorderly, the poor don't really have any explicit rights within Mallaby's system. The fact that they are disorderly or dysfunctional poses a threat to the rich and orderly societies. That threat is enough to justify the response of imperialism.

The reluctance that modifies the imperialism, therefore, has to do with an instrumental calculation of the various costs and benefits from this process. It has little or nothing to do with an ethical responsibility of one political community to another, of the Self to the Other. Additionally, the calculation of these costs and benefits has the rich and the orderly as the primary subjects and pays little attention to the costs for the poor and the disorderly.

What understanding of global governance undergirds this system? If participation in self-governance and the right to dissent are important aspects of any democratic order, then it is clear that those who are differentiated as poor or disorderly have no access to such rights. Those nations that lack wealth or order are denied democratic rights. Whatever the substantive conception of the global is here, it is not one that requires the consent of those who are to be ordered and governed.

How representative are Mallaby's opinions of the broader discourse on global governance? After September 11, such assertions about imperialism as a desirable mode of global governance don't appear to be unusual at all in the Anglo-Saxon parts of the Western world. Robert Cooper, a British diplomat and adviser to Prime Minister Tony Blair, has, for nearly similar reasons, also called for a "new kind of imperialism." Martin Wolf, a columnist for the *Financial Times* (London), builds on some of Cooper's work and Blair's speeches to also justify the need for a new imperialism.

It is easy to read the claims of Mallaby, Walker, and Cooper as colonial because they so explicitly demand a new imperialism. There is not much of an argument there, but I would assert that this is also a limited reading. The claims they make emerge from a liberal-colonial imaginary not just because they invoke imperialism explicitly but primarily because of a deeper disregard for the Other. It is obvious that Mallaby's reasoning concerns itself very little with either the rights of or costs to the poor. But what about those who appear to be more directly concerned about the poor?

In a speech to the British Labour Party, Tony Blair, for instance, laid out some worthy political principles—democracy, freedom, and justice—that should, in his view, structure global governance.[9] He offered an expanded conception of freedom as "not only in the narrow sense of personal liberty but in the broader sense of each individual having the economic and social freedom to develop their potential to the full," and he portrayed community as "founded on the equal worth of all. The starving, the wretched, the dispossessed, the ignorant, those living in want and squalor from the deserts of Northern Africa to the slums of Gaza, to the mountain ranges of Afghanistan: they too are our cause. This is a moment to seize." Surely, unlike Mallaby, this was a leader concerned with the global poor?

I would argue, however, that Blair is not too different from Mallaby in his disregard for the Other. If we agree, along with Blair, that democracy, freedom, and justice are desirable political principles that should underlie global governance, shouldn't we be finding ways to ensure that "the starving, the wretched, the dispossessed, the ignorant, those living in want and squalor from the deserts of Northern Africa to the slums of Gaza, to the mountain ranges of Afghanistan" somehow have a voice in these deliberations about them? Wouldn't we expect that political participation, the coconstitution of global order by the rich and the starving, by the blessed and the wretched, by the fortunate and the dispossessed, by the ignorant and the educated would be the first priority of those who sought to reorder the globe to facilitate freedom and community? But these constituencies do not have a say in such matters. They are only there as Blair's "cause," as somebody's "moment to seize."

A reasonably democratic order—at global or local levels—would support a politics that promotes the participation of those who are the objects of that policy. But what we get with Mallaby and Blair is global governance without the voice, consent, or participation of those who are to be governed. It is this deeper disregard for the Others that makes both Mallaby and Blair complicit in the production of a colonial mode of governance.

A similar colonial imaginary is apparent in the discourse of the

Bush administration. At first sight, the claims advanced by the officials of the Bush administration appear to leave some space for the political resolution of different imaginations of the global. Nicholas Lemann, Washington correspondent for the *New Yorker*, writes about asking Richard Haas, the director of policy planning for the State Department, whether there was a "successor idea to containment." Haas observes:

> It is the idea of integration. The goal of U.S. foreign policy should be to persuade the other major powers to sign on to certain key ideas as to how the world should operate: opposition to terrorism and weapons of mass destruction, support for free trade, democracy, markets. Integration is about locking them into these policies and then building institutions that lock them in even more. (Lemann 2002, 46)

Noteworthy here are a couple of things. First of all, the "key ideas" about "how the world should operate" are more or less set by the United States. They are not open to contestation. Politics is confined to the question of persuading others, primarily major powers, to "sign on," but even these major powers are not immune from U.S. coercion. As Haas reminds us, integration is about "locking them" into certain policies and ensuring that they cannot get out by "lock[ing] them in even more" through institutions.

So even in a case involving governance among major powers, the scope of politics is narrowly limited to an agreement about already decided "ideas" about "how the world should operate." Once they agree, an institutionalization of these policies further restricts the agency of these major powers. Those who seek to escape such institutionalizations run the risk of being seen as irresponsible or as outlaw or rogue states that fall outside this already limited domain of politics. Haas points out, for instance, that in the Bush administration's emerging "body of ideas" sovereignty "entails obligations" and has limits. Governments that fail to meet these obligations of sovereignty—"not to massacre your own people," "not to support terrorism in any way"—lose the "right to be left alone inside [their] territory." "Other governments," Haas asserts, "gain the right to intervene" (Lemann 2002, 46). This reconceptualization of national sovereignty is interesting to the extent that sovereignty is not the fundamental right of states anymore but rather a responsibility defined in some fairly specific, and even potentially commendable, ways. The responsibilities prescribed for the states themselves are not the problem. What is problematic is the presumption that they can come into being through the power of the Bush administration.

What is the basis of this power? Is it purely coercive or is it based on sound interpretations of the world? The relevant question then is on what basis does the Bush administration decide "how the world should operate"? Lemann points out that Bernard Lewis and Fouad Ajami are the outside experts on the Middle East—to take one region—who have the most credibility within the Bush administration. And what is their advice to members of the Bush administration on the Middle East? According to Lemann's source, Lewis presumably counseled the senior foreign policy members that "in that part of the world, nothing matters more than resolute will and force."

Those who possess interpretive power for "that part of the world" are advising those who hold coercive power that violence rather than deliberation makes for an effective politics with those who live there. The conjuncture between coercive and interpretive power could not be more complete in this specific case. As Assia Djebar reminds us, "And words themselves become a decoration, flaunted by officers like the carnations they wear in their buttonholes; words will become their most effective weapons. Hordes of interpreters, geographers, ethnographers, linguists, botanists, diverse scholars and professional scribblers will swoop down on this new prey. The supererogatory protuberances of their publications will form a pyramid to hide the initial violence from view" (1993, 45).

APPROPRIATING THE OTHER

In a scathing critique of the Bush administration's new grand strategy, John Ikenberry (2002) contrasts its unilateral drive unfavorably with the more historical grand strategies followed by earlier administrations. Specifically, he criticizes the "neoimperial vision" underlying the new grand strategy, a vision in which "the United States arrogates to itself the global role of setting standards, determining threats, using force, and meting out justice." While I take the overall point of Ikenberry's critique, I also find it to be typical of the sort of analysis that does not take the politics of meaning seriously and hence ends up unable to see a similar imperial or colonial nature in earlier, seemingly more multilateral U.S. strategies. It is with a view to highlighting that underlying colonial drive in U.S. engagements with Others in general that I closely read the Clinton White House's

1999 report "A National Security Strategy for a New Century,"[10] a good example of that earlier strategy. That report illustrates very well how the meanings of the global can be subordinated to the national even in the discourse of multilateralism. It appears, on the surface, to set a different tone from the Bush report. It begins by quoting Franklin Delano Roosevelt on the "lessons" that have been "learned" in terms of "global interdependence" and being "citizens of the world" and "members of the human community," but a careful reading of the text quickly reveals how many of the meanings of the global are carefully subverted to serve the national moment. The report presents a "global world" as one where there are Americans and there are Others. Americans ought to learn to be "citizens of the world," but this does not mean that they need to see themselves as equal to or like other "members of the human community." Being a citizen of the world implies primarily an awareness on the part of Americans that events happening "half-way around the earth" could affect their "safety, prosperity and their way of life."

Given this realization, Americans must acknowledge that they stand to benefit when other nations cooperate to tackle common problems. But the United States alone retains the primary responsibility for maintaining certain universal values and for guaranteeing global peace and prosperity. The United States entrusts itself with the responsibility for utilizing the "opportunities of this new global era" for its "own people" and "people around the world." We don't know—because the discourse doesn't tell us—what the views of others in the world are on such matters. The discourse does not, it appears, speak for "citizens of the world, members of the human community" who are not Americans.

What is clear, however, is what the discourse empowers in terms of identities, interests, and social practices. First of all, the discourse works to *appropriate* the global to service the interests of the U.S. state and the American nation in a number of ways, but primarily by creating a hierarchy of people in the world: those who are Americans and those who are not. The interests, practices, and concerns of Americans are central within this discourse. Classifying certain values as universal and others as particular, it sees globalization as the spread of these universal values but also moves to quickly appropriate them as always already American. Clearly there is no disjuncture here between the global and the national.

Second, the discourse marginalizes those who are not American in terms of their identities and practices by rarely lending voice or agency to other "members of the human community" or other "citizens of the world." The places these people inhabit are generally of relevance to the United States to the extent that they can provide opportunities, furnish imitators, resolve problems, or endanger U.S. interests and security, but they do not matter beyond that.

Third, the discourse treats difference in ways that consolidate the Self but that never validate it in its own right. Others matter primarily as reflections of the Self—actors who are or want to be like the United States. So the global "community of nations" that is invoked within the discourse is not a community that has a rich array of commonalty and difference. It is a community that is defined primarily as a "community of nations that share our interests." If social actors happen not to share American interests, they are excluded from the global community invoked within this discourse. There is no place for differences in interests here.

Finally, the global or universal values that are valorized within this discourse are not only appropriated as American but also treated as instrumental. Democracy, human rights, and respect for the rule of law are not necessarily good in themselves. You do not, for instance, see them being defended because of their intrinsic value. There is little or no talk of extending democracy from national to global levels, nor is it linked to the presence and promotion of difference within a truly global community. Values such as democracy are presented as good because they act as signs of the American Self and because they promote American interests.

As a result, within this imaginary, the global is consistently colonized by the American national. Global security is the security of the U.S. state and nation. The security of other people and other states is primarily a means toward this end. Global norms are derivative of the United States' core values and/or somehow useful for U.S. security and interests. The global community is essentially one that has interests similar to those of the United States. Global governance is not the result of a truly democratic process but essentially the acceptance of U.S. leadership by the rest of the world.

5

Productions of the Global

In March 1999, President Clinton, on a visit to Guatemala, regretted the role the United States had played in fostering its thirty-six-year civil war, admitting that it had been "wrong" in supporting a "brutal counterinsurgency campaign that slaughtered thousands of civilians."[1] Such expressions of regret notwithstanding, Clinton also firmly turned down the requests of Central American countries to "cease or slow" the deportation of many undocumented Central Americans from the United States. Against the pleas of these countries that these people were the source of desperately needed remittances, Clinton asserted that it was important to "discourage illegal immigration" and to "enforce our laws."

Four years later, in March 2003, Jose Antonio Gutierrez became the second U.S. marine to die in Iraq. Though a U.S. marine, Gutierrez was not an American citizen but a street child from Guatemala City, one of those thousands who had been orphaned during the Guatemalan civil war. He was also, in fact, one among the reportedly fifty thousand street children and teenagers who cross illegally into the United States every year.[2] Extolling his sacrifices for the nation, the U.S. government granted American citizenship to Gutierrez posthumously.

Understanding the human connections between the Self and the Other, the foreigner and the national, the legal/documented and the illegal/undocumented never seems to come on time. Occasionally, it comes with an apology in hand, an understanding and an apology that come after many hundreds of thousands—at least two hundred thousand in Guatemala to take only one figure—have been slaughtered, after many millions have been killed, well after, as one writer observes poignantly, the "orphans have grown up and the widows are dead or discouraged."[3]

Why this disjuncture, this perennial delay, this tardiness, in the understanding of such connections? How is it that we cannot see these human-global connections between the Self and the Other in the present? What allows a state to celebrate a marine in death, to wrap his sacrificial remittances within its borders even as it erases its violent complicity in orphaning him and pushing him beyond the borders of home and family in his all-too-brief life? How are states able to appropriate the death of a Gutierrez even as they make lives such as his a living hell?

Part of the problem here is obviously the amnesia induced by the original myth, in conventional international relations scholarship, of the nation-state as an autonomous and not always already global political space. Rather than asking what forms of globality historically connect and separate us, international relations assumes autonomous national selves and then gravely puzzles over the cooperative or conflictual properties of these socially impoverished beings. Occasionally, when our mutual relations become impossible to hide, they are transformed into questions about the novelty or the instability of these ties that bind. Hence it is an erasure, a willful form of "transnational [il]literacy" (Spivak in Landry and Maclean 1996) about the multiple connections that already exist, about the globalities that link Self and Other, the documented and the undocumented, the orphan and the citizen, that makes this routine lapse into illusory, autonomous selves possible.

I am not denying, by any means, the power of a world organized into an international system. But that organization is premised on the deliberate reconfiguration of earlier globalities, of a politically charged forgetting of an understanding of ourselves as the products of "overlapping territories and intertwined histories" (Said 1994). Moreover, what also reproduces this amnesia, this patchy memory, is our constant speaking of the world, as Arundhati Roy expressed it so felicitously, through the "languages of bankers and businessmen and politicians and generals."[4] Those languages are powerful and capable of producing or transforming very particular forms of globality, but they also produce an excess that might be worth seizing on, worth rearticulating in politically creative ways. In what follows, I trace some specific productions of the global and the politics that they empower in international relations.

GLOBAL RELAYS

Recent newspaper reports, based on figures from the U.S. Defense Department, indicate that noncitizens make up between 2.0 to 2.6 percent of the United States' active military personnel. Not only were these numbers portrayed as growing, but noncitizens were also seen as more likely to be in the line of fire.[5] On the other side of the battlefield, the *Washington Post* points out that of the 650,000 physicians in the United States, 160,000 are "international medical graduates" (i.e., approximately 25 percent of all U.S. physicians), and of these, 26,000 are from India (i.e., approximately 4 percent of all U.S. physicians and 16 percent of all international medical graduates).[6] But it also notes that "[i]mmigrant doctors now serve many of the most needy patient populations in the United States. They staff the clinics and hospitals . . . serving the inner cities and rural areas—jobs that many native-born doctors will not do."[7]

One way of understanding this imbrication of foreign bodies into U.S. domestic space is to read it as a function of objective forces of global demand and supply. A demand for skilled labor from within the United States is matched by a supply of unemployed but highly skilled workers from various parts of the world—a simple case of supply meeting demand. Though plausible, that reading misses out on the rich lode of politics—individual, local, national, international—that is involved. Supply doesn't introduce itself to demand in an objective space called the global economy. Is it coincidental that one country in the world supplies nearly 4 percent of all U.S. physicians? Or that one region within that country—not necessarily the most developed region within India by any means[8]—supplies a disproportionately high share, on some accounts more than three-fifths, of all Asian-American software engineers within the United States?

Using India as an example, I suggest that it is not accidental that foreignness is imbricated so deeply into America's economic spaces. How is it then that there is a sustained flow that links otherwise remote local spaces within India to those within the United States?

One answer, I would argue, lies in the politics that are productive of the social meanings, identities, and economic practices within India and the United States.

Let me illustrate this by returning to the story of A.P. Inc. Chandrababu Naidu, as I noted earlier, believes in globalizing Andhra Pradesh and in adopting a managerial approach to the governance of that region. Not surprisingly, the language of globality that one hears from Naidu has a very particular form involving terms such as "economic restructuring," "competitiveness," and "leadership" in the global economy. That language has also materialized itself in transformations of the built environment in Andhra Pradesh's capital city, Hyderabad, not least in the mission statements of places such as Hyderabad's Software Technology Park.[9] There are other expressions of that materiality. Hyderabad's software exports have been booming, increasing annually for the past five years by 100 percent or more.[10] It currently has at least six universities and ten engineering colleges, not to mention scores of software-training schools.[11] Software training in Hyderabad, as one commentator noted wryly, is a "social pathology."[12] The city itself is being reconstituted as an attractive destination, a global economic node, in a number of ways, so much so that it is increasingly referred to as "Cyberabad" or "Cyber City."

Fifteen miles from the center of the city, the first phase of Chief Minister Naidu's dream project, Hyderabad Information Technology Engineering Consultancy City (HI-TECH City), has been completed. Advertised as a "techno township built like a computer: user friendly, upgradable," HI-TECH City is expected to transform Hyderabad's identity, to remake it as a part of America in India, as the Silicon Valley of India. It is a space with state-of-the-art facilities—including high-speed data communication networks, satellite earth stations, power plants, multimedia infrastructure, and so on—needed by software companies and engineering consultancy firms. Economic actors such as Microsoft, Oracle, Silicon Graphics, Tata-IBM, Motorola, and others all have a presence there. The state government has also helped establish, in Hyderabad, a "Center of Excellence in computer education and training" called the Indian Institute of Information Technology (IIIT). Conceived as an "industry-driven, industry-financed and industry-managed institution," the IIIT offers long-term and short-term courses in information technology. Major information technology companies such as Microsoft, IBM, and Oracle have also set up corporate schools to offer training in their areas of core competence and to provide technological, financial, and consulting support.

Hyderabad is thus being transformed in specific ways and is being fashioned into a crucial site for the reproduction of Indo-U.S. and other global flows. However, this fashioning comes about not as an objective process but as the outcome of an active, meaningful effort on the part of many players and is heavily contingent on other actors conversing with Andhra Pradesh.

For A.P. Inc. to succeed in transforming itself from a local site to a global one, one of the effects of U.S. economic and political practices, for example, must be to sustain at least some of the practices emanating from Naidu. In other words, if Naidu restructures his economic space with the expectation that the U.S. economy would provide certain opportunities, with or without the American government's permission, then the net effect of American politics—whether American politicians know or care about Naidu is irrelevant here—must be to meet those expectations. This is then a question not of intentions but of unintended though workable effects across vast geographical, cultural, and informational distances.

How can an intersubjective relay, a global conversation, occur across such distances? In order to illustrate, I return to the American Competitiveness Bill, the bill that was cause for much joy in Hyderabad when it was passed. What was the U.S. Senate thinking in passing it? Did they necessarily want to make Hyderabadis happy by passing this act? A brief examination of the debate over the bill reveals some interesting contestations.

In opposition,[13] Senator Dianne Feinstein presented the bill as an issue that pitted national and local identities against foreign ones. This bill, she observed, would "permit 555,000 new 'foreign nationals' to come into this country—50 percent of whom would remain." The political issue, for Feinstein, was one of safeguarding the rights to an economic space. Nationals (those who are "graduates into the global economy from our schools all over the United States"), according to Feinstein, had a prior right to these "555,000 jobs." Feinstein's argument, in implicitly empowering nationals and disempowering foreign nationals, works on a commonsensical understanding of the contemporary international system as one in which nations and their nationals have sovereign rights over national economic spaces.

But Feinstein also seemed to believe in a global economy, an economic space that was greater than just the U.S. one. She pointed out, "these are exactly the jobs that graduates of the new age, graduates into the global economy from our schools all over the United States should be taking to develop a specialization in an industry which is only going to bloom in the future."

What does it mean to restrict foreigners in the national economic space even as one tries to get nationals into a global economy? How are national rights distributed within global economic spaces? Why would a global economy be open only to graduates from U.S. schools and not to those from other nations? Feinstein, it seems, subscribes to a conception of the United States both as a national economic space, within which the particularity of U.S. national identity is privileged, and as part of a global economic space into which U.S. graduates could be fed. This contradiction of a global that simultaneously sees itself as national is, as explained before, understandable in terms of the liberal-colonial imaginary of the United States.

How did supporters of the bill articulate their claims? Senator John McCain, in cosponsoring the bill, began by differentiating between what the bill appeared to be about ("it deals ostensibly with the visa cap on foreign-born hi-tech workers") and its presumably "far more profound" "effect" of "enhanc[ing] the competitiveness of the American economy at a time when U.S. companies, if given access to the necessary resources, are poised to dominate the Information Age for decades to come."[14] McCain's claims are significant first and foremost for the way they sought to problematize any Feinsteinian reading of the bill as about immigration. Read as a bill about immigration, the debate would rely on the dominant understanding of the international system as structured on the principle of the rights of nations over specific territorial spaces. That would mean a debate over the relative rights of the foreign-born over nationals. But McCain foreclosed such a reading by arguing that the bill was about American competitiveness in the global economy rather than about letting in foreign-born high-tech workers. In other words, he rearticulated the contradiction of supporting a global economy but also defending specific rights over national economic spaces.

Turning his attention away from U.S. nationals to corporations, he noted that the bill would help U.S. companies succeed in the global economy. McCain's argument changed the subject; the signs of Americanness were no longer attached to the workers but located at the level of companies. Not to let in skilled foreign workers, McCain argued, would hurt American companies and their employees, and that was not in the public interest. The workers were back in the picture now but as subsidiaries to American companies. The context shifted, as a result of this articulation, from a focus on the public interest at stake in the competition between workers in the global economy to that involved in the competition between corporations in the global economy.[15]

The supporters argued that the bill was not just about competitiveness but also about being competitive enough to ensure that the United States remained the number one power. This was the winning argument because the opposition to the bill functioned within the imaginative and interpretive parameters of a global economy and American identity as number one. It did not question such articulations by asking, What exactly was sacrosanct about a global economy? or Why should the U.S. have to be number one (especially if it meant that its nationals had to suffer)? Feinstein, for example, did not intervene to ask why the Senate should really care about the global economy or about the United States being number one if, in the process, U.S. jobs were lost or U.S. nationals were replaced by foreigners.

The claim that passing the bill would ensure the maintenance of an American identity as number one silenced the opposition by invoking another social claim that was not easily questionable. It was not that McCain and other supporters of the bill were much more internationalist while Feinstein was an isolationist. All three talked in the name of the United States, of American society, and of American public interests. But implicit in their arguments was a contest over how America was to be defined and who would be empowered through such a definition. Within the articulations of the supporters, U.S. companies needed access to "foreign-born hi-tech workers," even at the cost of local- and national-born workers, in order to maintain an American identity of being number one.

McCain's claims situated Americans as multiple social actors, but empowered only some of them while disempowering others. For instance, his characterization presented those Americans who were not filling these high-tech jobs as making an agentic choice. Americans were not filling these jobs because they did not want to ("jobs Americans are not filling"; "jobs Americans cannot and do not fill"). He did not ask why Americans were not doing so or whether there were ways in which they could be encouraged to do so. In other words, his articulation resisted any structural interpretation of the problem. American consumers who benefited from the efficient production of goods, and two non-American groups, skilled professionals and those who bought American exports overseas, were also empowered discursively. But the most empowered were those "U.S. companies that can set up shop in India, Pakistan, Costa Rica."[16]

The bill was necessary because these social actors would otherwise leave ("I support this bill because I do not wish to encourage more U.S. companies to set up shop in India, Pakistan, Costa Rica, and other sources of skilled labor unavailable in sufficient quantities in the United States. I support this bill because I do not think a job is better going unfilled than going to an educated foreign national on a temporary visa to the United States.")[17] The power of these corporations to cross a territorially demarcated national space called America and still remain American was never called into question within McCain's articulation.[18]

When opponents questioned the power of such groups, they did so in a very limited fashion. They problematized the right of these companies to determine who came into the privileged space of the U.S. national economy. In doing this, they kept reverting to an assertion of rights within the framework of a nationally structured economic system. But that was not a conception that they held onto fully either. They asserted national rights over economic spaces but also sought to hold onto the idea of a global economy in which the United States was number one. Their articulations thus failed to push or rearticulate the boundaries of the politically imaginable while conceding the dominant identity and definitions of the international system to their opponents.

There were some prominent taken-for-granteds in the Senate debate. These included conceptions of what American national identity was (being number one), the nature of the international system (a global economy), the supply of an essential resource for American competitiveness (skilled foreigners), the demand for such a resource from U.S. companies (the availability of high-tech jobs), the critical nature of this resource for the continued competitiveness of the American economy, and the relative willingness or inability of Americans to fill those jobs in the specified time frame. Left unquestioned were the willingness of U.S. companies to move from U.S. shores if the desired supply was not forthcoming and what factors were within political control. The debate treated territorial America and the legislators' control over it as an important power to be deployed. The competitiveness of companies, the competitiveness of workers, and the "distribution and reapportionment of rights within national economic space" were other social powers seen as susceptible to political manipulation and control.

It is critical to understand that none of the factors that were taken for granted—American identity as number one, a global economy, an unfulfilled quota of high-tech jobs—were essentially outside of political control. One could disagree about the degree of government control or the relevant time horizons for policy manipulation, but not their very availability for manipulation. In other words, it was possible to imagine, plan, and act politically for a world in which the United States need not be committed to the idea of always being number one; it was possible to imagine, plan, and act politically for a world that ought not to be a global economy; it was possible to imagine, plan, and act politically to meet the unfilled quota of high-tech jobs from a national territorial base rather than from other nations. Such issues were not outside of politics, only outside of political contestation. I am not arguing that the government or the legislators could articulate anything they wanted, only that the decision to portray some actions as outside of one's control was a function of politics, not of reality. That portrayal, in that sense, was itself an act of politics.

Whatever the politically open-ended nature of economic policy, the net effect of passing the American Competitiveness Bill was to reproduce at least some of those expectations that went into Naidu's economic restructuring efforts. By increasing the quota of H-1B workers allowed into the United States, the U.S. government helped to sustain at least one set of flows between two local spaces in the international system. It also reproduced the social powers of two sets of deterritorialized actors: the corporations that threatened to move and the people who would be entering into the United States on H-1B visas to work for these companies.

Does this mean that there is a shared language of globalization? That effective coordination of this sort is equivalent to the unintended harmonization and convergence of economic policies? I agree that the vocabulary of restructuring—competitiveness, for instance—is common enough to be present in many places, but the languages of globality are not quite exhausted by such terms.

Let me illustrate this by turning to Naidu again. Addressing a retreat of civil servants, Naidu talked the talk, deploying the language of competition and economic restructuring and asserting that economic reforms necessarily entailed the "state yielding to the market" in some areas.[19] But he also rearticulated the language of this globality. He spoke explicitly of allowing a large and important role for government in areas where markets failed. He saw "market failure" as "axiomatic" in some cases. He asserted that his government was not withdrawing from its responsibilities to the poor but emphasizing them and wanted to invest massively in infrastructure developments. In other words, while deploying the discourse of a particular globality, Naidu also drew a different lesson from it: greater government responsibility rather than lesser.

In a different instance, talking about the vital role played by information technology in improving the competitiveness of the national economy, the government of Andhra Pradesh's National Informatics Policy Submission Paper asserted that much of the "information content on international networks relate to the developed countries of the West. Network connectivity can therefore have connotations of cultural imperialism unless steps [are] taken to develop indigenous information in the country to maintain national culture and identity."[20]

"Cultural imperialism"? "indigenous information"? One would have thought that these terms belonged to the era of the New International Economic Order (NIEO) and not Naidu's globalizing era. But how did such claims find their way into the language of a politician who is the toast of the World Bank? This was definitely not an idiosyncratic choice of Naidu's. It is a more systemic presence that leaves its traces everywhere in the discourse of economic restructuring in India.

Such a presence was also evident in how legislators in the Andhra Pradesh legislative assembly debated Microsoft's entry into Hyderabad. A Communist Party of India (Marxist) member cautioned the chief minister about the perils of welcoming multinationals into the state, reminding him of the Indian experience with the East India Company. The BJP leader agreed and argued that the profits of Microsoft should not be allowed to be repatriated back to the United States. A Congress member regretted that the state was in a situation where the importance of foreigners and the World Bank was growing. The left, right, and centrist parties thus continued to function well within the parameters of a postcolonial Indian identity dominated by concerns about colonialism.

How then are we to understand the scope of the languages constitutive of the dominant understandings of locality, nationality, and globality? I intend to highlight a couple of examples in which the social meanings available in the languages of globality were rearticulated in politically creative ways.

INTERRUPTIONS

Speaking at the commencement ceremony of the U.S. Coast Guard on May 17, 2000, President Clinton observed that "[g]lobalization [was] tearing down barriers and building new networks among nations and people." But, he cautioned, there was also a downside to this process. These "new networks" also gave rise to new insecurities. He noted, "The same technology that gave us GPS [Global Positioning System] and the . . . Internet also apparently empowered a student sitting in the Philippines to launch a computer virus that . . . spread through more than 10 million computers and caused billions of dollars in damage." This combination of a new openness and new insecurities signaled a "fateful struggle" between the "forces of integration and harmony" and the "forces of disintegration and chaos."[21]

Listening to Clinton one might be tempted to believe that the Filipino students who unleashed this virus represented the "forces of disintegration and chaos," and that, like the protesters in Seattle and Washington, they were opposed to globalization and this was their way of showing their destructive potential. Or maybe it was just an accident that most Filipinos regretted. But it was increasingly evident that Filipinos neither resented globalization nor showed any contrition at the damage done by the spread of the "ILOVEYOU" computer virus. What was evident was joy and nationalist pride at the power of the virus. At least some Filipino newspaper columnists diagnosed the virus as a symptom of the technical prowess and ingenuity of Filipino students. The creator of the program was seen by others as a national hero. By unleashing the virus, he had managed, one prominent columnist noted, to "put the Philippines on the world map" and had "proven that the Filipino has the creativity and ingenuity to turn, for better or for worse, the world upside down."[22]

Under existing national regulations, the launch of the computer virus was not a crime since the Philippines did not have laws regulating cybercrimes. Although there was no legal basis to treat it as a crime, one would surely expect to see some widely shared global norms that understood causing damage to the work and property of others as a deplorable act or, at least, as something unworthy of celebration. Contrary to such expectations, many Filipinos appeared to have fairly ambiguous feelings about this "crime." One student, for example, asserted that it was "wrong," but he could not help seeing it also as an "amazing" feat. Another student observed: "Can you imagine, they were able to penetrate the Pentagon? Even though the Philippines is a third-world country, even though we're behind in technology, they were able to do that."[23] Other commentators noted that the creators of the computer program had achieved two useful tasks: guaranteed themselves great jobs in the global computer industry and drawn the world's attention to the computer skills available in the Philippines. In other words, far from committing a crime, they had performed a great service to themselves and their country!

If we believe, along with Clinton, that the "ILOVEYOU" computer virus represented a new *global* threat, how do we understand its celebration in a third world country? How does a global threat transform itself into a celebratory act merely by crossing national borders?

State officials and conventional scholars of international relations might argue that computer viruses represent real security threats in a globalizing world. While such an act might not be a crime in many countries, it needs to be seen as one given its considerable destructive potential. Following this line of argument, they might point to the need for a global coordination of cyberlaws so that people all over the world would recognize and treat the spreading of computer viruses as a global crime. Though correct in identifying the loopholes in existing laws concerning global transactions, such an explanation would not take us very far. It does not, for instance, tell us why many Filipinos were celebrating an act that, while not illegal in their country, was quite destructive in its effects.

Were the Filipino students motivated by anti-American sentiments or were they against globalization in any form? There is little or no evidence to suggest either. What evidence we have suggests, instead, that the Filipino students were actually on the side of greater globalization, that they wanted to join the global economy, and that many of their compatriots saw the spread of the virus as actually increasing their chances of joining the global economy. How do we account then for the celebration and pride of the Filipinos in their capacity to destroy a global order that they would rather join?

Such a difference in the national understandings of specific actions is not an entirely new phenomenon in the contemporary international system. The nuclear tests conducted by India and Pakistan demonstrated a similar disjuncture of imaginations. While many in the first world saw them as heralding a more dangerous world and as increasing global insecurity, many others in the third world, particularly in India and Pakistan, saw it as a sign of technical competence and state agency. Mainstream scholars have sought to explain those actions as driven, somehow, by real threats, but such explanations are fairly limited in their explanatory power.[24]

Disjunctures such as these demonstrate the complex sedimentations—the historically institutionalized layers of social meanings, identities, and interests—evoked and involved in the construction and dissemination of various languages of globality. In the case of cybersecurity, Filipino voices interrupt and complicate any attempt to constitute a global order unilaterally. It is precisely the distant and powerful nature of this regime that tempts subaltern actors to demonstrate their agency by interrupting it. Ignored, disregarded, and denied voice and coauthorship in the constitution of global orders, subaltern actors take pleasure in their power to rescript these orders, however perverse the effects, from the margins.

AMBIVALENCE AND CO-OPTION

Along with the Nuclear Non-proliferation Treaty (NPT) and the Fissile Material Cut-off Treaty (FMCT), the Comprehensive Test Ban Treaty (CTBT) forms a triad of international treaties put in place to manage and regulate issues of nuclear security. In what follows I focus on the international efforts to institutionalize and bring into effect one of these treaties, the CTBT.

The CTBT is an international treaty that bans "all nuclear explosions." This ban is intended to "constrain the development and qualitative improvement of all nuclear weapons," "end the development of advanced new types of nuclear weapons," "contribute to the prevention of nuclear proliferation and the process of nuclear disarmament," and, by doing all this, "strengthen international peace and security." Pursuing these goals, the CTBT seeks to put in place a "verification regime" consisting of an "International Monitoring System (IMS)" with seismological, radionuclide, hydroacoustic, and infrasound monitoring facilities located in a worldwide network of member states. The verification regime authorizes practices of "On-Site Inspections (OSI)," "consultation and clarification," and "confidence building measures." The treaty also creates an organization— the CTBTO—to foresee the implementation and verification of these goals and provides for "measures . . . to ensure compliance, including sanctions." The CTBT is of "unlimited duration," though each state has the "right to withdraw from the CTBT if it decides that extraordinary events related to its subject matter have jeopardized its supreme national interests."[25] When the UN General Assembly voted on September 10, 1996, to adopt the CTBT, then U.S. secretary of state Warren Christopher explicitly posited a conjuncture between the CTBT, the security of the United States, and the security of "every nation in the world." The CTBT, he claimed, was a global security structure that "demonstrate[d] the power of the international community to unite around a great goal, and to act together to improve the security of all its members."[26]

The CTBT appears to be a global security structure, presumably institutionalizing certain globally shared norms and based on the well-negotiated and informed consent of states in the international system. It would seem easy then to agree with John D. Holum, acting undersecretary of state for arms control and international security affairs and director, U.S. Arms Control and Disarmament Agency, that "Even before it has entered into force, the Comprehensive Nuclear-Test Ban Treaty has created a nearly *universal* expectation that countries will not conduct nuclear test explosions."[27]

After all, if a treaty commanded the voluntary assent of more than 160 states and enshrined their shared norms on nuclear explosions and testing, could it not be seen as enjoying a certain universal expectation or widespread normative power? I would claim, however, that if we conceptualized the CTBT purely as a global norm about to be institutionalized, we miss an important aspect of the politics that has gone into its universal institutionalization. A more careful analysis of the CTBT presents an extremely interesting puzzle: Though the treaty presents itself as institutionalizing seemingly universal norms on nuclear testing, its impending enactment actually encouraged a deliberate, repeated, and dramatic violation of those very universal expectations by different states. Only after intentionally violating these ostensibly shared norms did different states rush to swear their future commitment to it.

TEST AND SIGN

On August 10, 1993, the Geneva Conference on Disarmament (CD) gave its Ad Hoc Committee on a Nuclear Test Ban the authority to begin negotiations on a CTBT. Less than two months later, on October 5, 1993, China conducted a nuclear test, its first since Clinton's appeal for a global moratorium on testing. The White House issued a statement regretting China's decision to test. On December 16, 1993, the UN General Assembly passed a resolution, by consensus, supporting the multilateral negotiation of a CTBT. CTBT negotiations began in the ad hoc committee in January 1994. Soon thereafter, on June 13, 1995, France announced that it would resume nuclear testing in the South Pacific in September of that year. The White House issued a statement regretting France's decision to test.

In December 1995, as the UN General Assembly (UNGA) passed, again by consensus, a resolution asking the CD to conclude the CTBT soon, India made its own plans to conduct a nuclear test, which would have been its first in twenty-one years. The test was called off when its preparations were detected and India came under intense pressure from the United States. China conducted yet another nuclear test on July 29, 1996, and declared a moratorium on nuclear testing the next day.

A little more than a month later, on September 10, 1996, the UNGA voted to adopt the CTBT and open it for signature at the earliest possible date by a vote of 158 in favor, 3 opposed, and 5 abstentions. Clinton became the first world leader to sign the CTBT on

September 24, 1996, but only after ensuring that the CTBT, while prohibiting all nuclear explosions, did not prohibit "all activities involving a release of nuclear energy." This meant that the United States was free to conduct subcritical tests. The United States also took care to ensure that the prohibitions in Article I of the CTBT did not apply "to the use of nuclear weapons in the event of war."[28] In other words, if the United States or any other state ended up using nuclear weapons in war, the resulting explosions would not count as a violation of the CTBT. Following its signature on the CTBT, on July 2, 1997, the U.S. Department of Energy conducted the first in a series of subcritical tests. The tests continued into late March 1998. At least fifteen countries (including Norway, Indonesia, Mexico, Malaysia, Iran), the mayors of Hiroshima and Nagasaki, forty-six members of the U.S. Congress, many NGOs engaged in disarmament movements, and the European Parliament condemned the subcritical tests of the United States as "violating the spirit" of the CTBT.[29] Understood legally, none of the states that had tested so far had broken any law. They had only violated the spirit of the CTBT. But such violations of the spirit of the CTBT only increased in the future.

On May 11, 1998, twenty-four years after its first nuclear test in May 1974, India announced that it had successfully conducted three nuclear tests. The United States condemned the tests and warned that it was reviewing the imposition of trade and financial sanctions on India. Less than twelve hours after the U.S. warning, and almost as if in response, the Indian government followed up with two more tests on May 13. Subsequently, the Indian government expressed its commitment to "a total, global elimination of nuclear weapons" and to "some form of participation" in the CTBT on the basis of "reciprocity." Seventeen days later, first on May 28 and then on May 30, Pakistan conducted its own set of nuclear tests. Soon thereafter, it also expressed its commitment to joining the CTBT.

A strictly legalistic interpretation of the race to test and commit, as I pointed out earlier, leaves little room for condemning the actions of these states. None of the states that conducted nuclear tests—not even India and Pakistan—broke any international law or any treaty that they had signed. They were accused of violating, however, something termed "the spirit" of the CTBT. Understood conceptually, what is this spirit of the CTBT?

THE SPIRIT OF THE CTBT

If the spirit of the CTBT is a shared norm, a universal expectation, against conducting nuclear tests, how does one make sense of the actions of those states that tested and then committed themselves to the CTBT? How does one explain the fairly indecent hurry of states to first systematically and deliberately offend the spirit of a shared value and then dedicate themselves to it? What sort of a shared norm is it that states rush to break before they swear any commitment to it?

Faced with such conceptual complications, some scholars have been quick to undermine the analytical utility of global norms and international laws and to reassert the importance of power and interests in the structuring of state practices. Fareed Zakaria argued, for instance, that the Indian and Pakistani nuclear tests had demolished a central myth that the contemporary world could be made safe through regimes such as the CTBT and NPT. In Zakaria's conceptualization, the "elaborate set of international treaties and laws" to control nuclear weapons did not have the power to constrain the self-interested and power-driven actions of states in the international system. International treaties and laws were so much "paperwork" that could not come in the way of "geopolitical realities."[30] Subsequent developments have also appeared to back such a position.

Indian security policy, on the other hand, offers a somewhat different entry into the social imaginations and relations of power that go into the constitution of the global. Ambivalence toward the global is the dominant theme. A close reading of the discourse of India's policy makers reveals a postcolonially imagined world of global security. The postcolonial imaginary is oriented toward the production of noncolonial global orders. As a result, it constantly resists efforts to reproduce global orders that function purely on colonial lines. But the postcolonial imaginary does not necessarily transform the resistance into a sustained anticolonial revolt either. Positioned between the colonizer and the colonized, splitting its sympathies with both, a postcolonial imaginary complicates, at best, the easy reproduction of colonial global orders.

India's 1998 decision to test nuclear weapons is a particularly apt manifestation of a postcolonial imaginary's ambivalence toward the institutionalization of a colonial order of governance. That decision, taken nearly a quarter century after India's first test, obstructed the efforts of the existing nuclear weapons states to institutionalize a global nuclear order structured around the NPT and the CTBT. The obstruction of the global nuclear order is particularly striking since India was one of the first countries to propose a CTBT. What is the source of this ambivalence?

The Indian state subscribed to the institutionalization of a global order in which there was a shared commitment against conducting nuclear explosions. This, however, was not a discrete commitment but intrinsically related to other powerful understandings of the role of nuclear weapons in the promotion of global insecurity that saw the likely use of nuclear weapons as "the gravest threat to humanity and to peace and stability in the international system." Thus global security entailed a total and complete elimination of nuclear weapons.

The CTBT's ban on nuclear testing was a value that held significance for Indian policy makers because of its power to advance this broader goal of the elimination of nuclear weapons. Without that linkage, India's policy makers argued, a treaty such as the CTBT would only legitimize, as the NPT had done before, an unequal world in which a few states had the right to maintain and refine their nuclear arsenals while others were placed under a mode of governance that ruled out similar rights for them. Such an unequal world was tolerable, in official Indian eyes, only if the states with nuclear weapons committed themselves to a time-bound program that eliminated their nuclear arsenals and brought them on par with the nonnuclear ones. This would constitute a really secure world: one in which no one had nuclear weapons or exclusive rights to them. That was the global order, India claimed, that must arise out of the complex set of treaties that were centered on the CTBT, the NPT, the FMCT, the Chemical Weapons Convention (CWC), and the Biological Weapons Convention (BWC).

The postcolonial understanding of global order was thus one in which all states gave up their right to nuclear weapons so that the world would be a more secure place—at least in terms of weapons of mass destruction. In that sense, India was explicitly committed to a global norm of not testing, though this was seen, primarily, as a way of attaining the eventual goal of eliminating nuclear weapons. The CTBT's significance for India lay not merely in its prevention of proliferation but in its ability to promote universal nuclear disarmament. The global dimension of security was connected to universal nuclear disarmament and not just the regime of nonproliferation.

One sign of this alternative imagination of global security lay in the fact that, as I mentioned earlier, India was one of the first countries to suggest the idea of a CTBT in 1954. India had also continued to campaign consistently for the total elimination of nuclear weapons and signed on, without any problems, to the CWC, which unlike the NPT and the CTBT was seen as a nondiscriminatory regime. India's international relations were structured to promote a CTBT that would advance the elimination of nuclear weapons, cap both vertical and horizontal proliferation, and show a clear path to the eventual elimination of nuclear weapons.

But the CTBT that was finally negotiated, in the Indian official view, fell far short of such an ambition because it only banned further testing. As the Indian minister for external affairs pointed out to the fiftieth session of the UN General Assembly: "It cannot be argued that the security of a few countries depends on their having nuclear weapons, and that of the rest depends on their not. . . . we note that Nuclear Weapon States have agreed to a CTBT only after acquiring the know-how to develop and refine their arsenals without the need for tests" (quoted in Ghose 1997, n.p.).

In the absence of any explicit linkages to other commitments about the elimination of nuclear weapons, the CTBT—the very treaty that India had championed consistently—took on a different meaning for Indian policy makers. As the Indian representative to the CD pointed out, "The CTBT that we see emerging . . . (is) not the CTBT India envisaged in 1954. This cannot be the CTBT that India can be expected to accept" (quoted in Ghose 1997, n.p.).

Far from being a benign commitment, the treaty against nuclear testing became a threatening sign of the growing power of the Permanent Five to institutionalize, against the wishes of many, a colonial nuclear order structured around their specific version of global security. The CTBT, in Indian eyes, appeared now as a system of nuclear apartheid, a regime that was seen as discriminatory in terms of its distribution of rights and duties between the "nuclear have-lots" and the "nuclear have-nots." The emerging global order thus presented a set of stark choices for Indian policy makers. As Jaswant Singh, India's minister of external affairs at the time, expressed it,

"India's nuclear policy remains firmly committed to a basic tenet: that the country's national security in a world of nuclear proliferation lies either in global disarmament or in exercise of the principle of equal and legitimate security for all."[31]

As "threshold" nuclear states that had demonstrated a nuclear capability but had not "weaponized" or asserted an overt nuclear identity, Israel, India, and Pakistan were positioned ambiguously in earlier global orders. But as the CTBT was being institutionalized, the legal and diplomatic space for the maintenance of such ambiguous identities became considerably less because the CTBT created two distinct sets of actors with different rights and responsibilities. One set of global actors—the nuclear "have-lots"—did not have to commit themselves to any eventual phasing out of nuclear weapons while another set—the nuclear "have-nots"—took on the added obligations of forswearing any further testing.

What did it signify, in the Indian national imagination, to be a member of one group or the other? Indian policy makers saw India becoming an "object" in the emerging global nuclear order if they did not assert their nuclear "subjectivity." If there is anything that a postcolonial imaginary resents and resists strongly, it is the seeming relapse into the position of a colonized object. India's 1998 tests are best read therefore as explicitly political acts that testified, as a commentator in *Le Monde* put it, to the "dry assertion of the existence of other visions of the world."[32] The tests were, in many ways, a refusal to accept the position of an object in an emerging global colonial order. They also signaled, ironically, an increasing willingness on the part of Indian policy makers to accept membership in a global order that they themselves condemned as colonial.

Conclusion
Resistance and Rearticulation

The end of the world begins not with the barbarians at the gate, but with the barbarians at the highest levels of the state. All the states in the world.

BEN OKRI, GUARDIAN

Between November and December 1999, as a prelude to the meeting of the World Trade Organization (WTO) in Seattle, a group of more than sixty NGOs brought out a series of full-page advertisements in the *New York Times*.[1] Each advertisement focused on one particular aspect of globalization and sought to show how that was advancing the interests of global corporations but not of countries.[2] I examine one of these ads—the first one in the series—as a way of indicating the limitations of some putatively radical alternatives to the dominant discourses of the global. I then read another critique—of received notions of nuclear security—to indicate the more progressive possibilities of other forms of resisting the global.

The first antiglobalization advertisement taken out by the NGOs was striking in devoting two full pages to its case.[3] The first page presented four rows of photographs, three pictures in each row, and underneath each picture was a question asking the reader to identify the place being shown. The first picture was an aerial view of highways with the query, "Is this Los Angeles or Cairo?" The other pictures were of rows of cars ("Is this Seoul or Detroit?"), the inside of an office with people working on computers ("Is this Atlanta or Tokyo?"), the inside of a poultry farm ("Is this California or Manchester?"), an aerial view of suburban houses ("Is this New Jersey or Caracas?"), two pipes emptying effluents into a canal ("Is this Arizona or Mexico?"), tree stumps in a deforested area ("Is this Maine or Sarawak?"), the inside of a department store ("Is this India or London?"), the outside of an apartment complex ("Is this St. Louis or Ukraine?"), a busy street with people dressed in suits ("Is this Wall St. or Buenos Aires?"), and a picture of high-rise buildings in a downtown area ("Is this Tokyo or Milan?"). The final picture depicted the golden arches of McDonald's with the caption, "Any answer will do." The second page textualized the visual essay of the first page. Titled "Global Monoculture," the text described the changes that had been wrought by economic globalization:

> A few decades ago, it was still possible to leave *home* and go *somewhere else*: the architecture was *different,* the landscape was *different,* the language, lifestyle, dress, and values were *different.* That was a time when we could speak of cultural diversity. But with economic globalization, diversity is fast disappearing. The goal of the global economy is that all countries should be homogenized. When global hotel chains advertise to tourists that all their rooms in every city of the world are identical, they don't mention that the cities are becoming identical too: cars, noise, smog, corporate high-rises, violence, fast-food, McDonald's, Nikes, Levis, Barbie Dolls, American TV and film. *What's the point of leaving home?* (Emphasis added)

What is the point of leaving home? What, one is also tempted to ask, is the point of contesting globalization if the underlying imagination is so impoverished in its implicit conception of political community and responsibility? If that conclusion appears too cryptic, allow me to elaborate.

Let us begin with the visual essay. The essay works if readers automatically associate some distinctive signs with different places. So for this ad to be convincing, Cairo must evoke pyramids and maybe camels in your mind rather than highways, which are stabilized as one of the markers of Los Angeles; Detroit, rather than Seoul, is equated with cars; New Jersey has suburbs, not Caracas; Mexico has pollutants flowing into rivers, not Arizona; London has department stores, not India. The politics of the ad revolves around arguing that this historically established binary of identity and difference, of Self and Other, of home and abroad, of domestic and foreign is now under threat of erasure from the homogenizing force of globalization. Globalization is threatening to erase the differences between "our" places and "theirs."

The places associated with home, with the Self, and with identity are being replaced by places that ought to look different but are in danger of not doing so. Cairo, Seoul, Tokyo, Ukraine, Buenos Aires, Manchester, and Caracas are threatening to turn into Los Angeles, Detroit, Atlanta, St. Louis, Wall Street, California, and New Jersey. But why should this be threatening? It is threatening because it reduces cultural diversity and makes it meaningless for "us" to leave "home." "What's the point," as the ad asks us, "of leaving home?" What, in other words, is the point of leaving "home" if we cannot be assured of being able to access (consume?) "difference" outside? Implicit in this articulation of resistance to economic globalization and its presumed homogenizing of the world are some very troubling assumptions of culture, identity, political community, and practice.

First, it is apparently the burden of some of us in the world to consume difference while others are condemned historically to supply that difference. One implication is that the "consumers" move but the "consumed" remain unchanged. Cairo must always be the place for camels and pyramids and never that of highways. India cannot become, cannot be imagined as, the site of department stores. These cities and countries are frozen in terms of certain common historically associated images and future possibilities.

Second, these Other places and nations do not figure in these images as having any agency. The NGOs do not ask whether Cairo might want highways like Los Angeles. They do not wonder if it would necessarily cease to be Cairo if it did construct highways. Would Caracas cease to have its identity if it developed suburbs similar to those in New Jersey? Maybe homogenization—in terms of the built environment, life opportunities, security, and health— may not be an unmitigated evil. Maybe Caracas, Buenos Aires, Mexico, India, Seoul want some degree of homogenization. Maybe they want to be, in some respects, like everyplace else. But the message rules that out as unthinkable, unimaginable. The NGOs essentially reverse the arguments of proglobalization advocates, such as Thomas Friedman, who assume, equally unreflectively, that other countries just want to become "America." One privileges difference, the other identity, but both fail to problematize the received notions of the national Self and the Other.

Third, the ad freezes these countries and places in time not necessarily because it is in their interests but because it is in "our" interests: "we," who could a "few decades ago . . . leave home and go somewhere else," are now finding it difficult to find places that are "different." Other nations existed for us as rich sources for the consumption of difference: language, architecture, landscape, lifestyle, dress, values. Now they have what we have. They have become us. So what's the point of leaving home? "Soon," the ad argues, "every place might be just like every place else." Oh, the horror, the horror!

Let us examine the critical potential of this articulation. More than sixty NGOs are signing onto a statement that offers an extremely thin conception of politics, culture, identity, and political practice. What could have been an important political struggle against unwanted forms of globalization is reduced to a fight to protect the privileged forms of consumption—of national difference—of a select few. What is the political principle underlying resistance to globalization here? That global corporations are threatening to destroy the capacity of some of us to consume national differences and hence they need to be resisted?

Implicit in this articulation is a very parochial conception of political solidarity. Political community is necessarily limited to the national "home." Each nation, each country is seen as discrete in its struggles. While alliances across one's national home are not ruled out, the discourse automatically sees the national border as marking the limits of responsibility, community, and accountability. Those who find this ad persuasive implicitly accept the boundaries of the national as the legitimate and primary realm for contesting dominant corporate productions of the global, and so they allow the imaginable and possible realms of political practice to be stunted by historically inherited national identities and privileges. They look primarily to their own nations in their struggles against globalization and implicitly expect other participants to do likewise.

They also appear to subscribe to an understanding of politics as a struggle to retain their existing rights to certain forms of consumption, which is a very restrictive assumption to make if one is interested in a critical struggle against globalization. What is forgotten, in the process, is that all nations are not necessarily equally privileged in the global distribution of assets and liabilities. A globalization that hurts the consumption interests of the historically well-to-do nations—especially in the areas of consuming difference—might not necessarily hurt the interests or disturb the sleep of the historically deprived. There is little in this imagination that can excite the solidarity of those who are not already well off or those who do not have a stake in consuming national differences. More than sixty NGOs have thus signed onto a statement that is oriented predominantly toward the production of a world in which some nations (and some nationals) still matter more than others. Their discourse offers colonial globality as emancipation—their emancipation.

Are our articulations of the global doomed then to the historical power and poverty of our colonial modern, exclusively national, imaginations? Not necessarily. Those concerned with political transformation can think about constituting the global in ways that are empowered by the national imaginations they inherit but also go beyond them in many important ways. Let me illustrate this with a critique of the dominant conception of the global on the issue of nuclear security.

Arundhati Roy, the Booker Prize–winning author of *The God of Small Things,* was an important critic of the Indian government's decision to conduct nuclear explosions in 1998. Going against the majority of Indian middle-class opinion, she wrote a scathing essay—titled *The End of Imagination* (1998)—criticizing the justifications offered by the Indian government. Characterizing the decision as "the final act of betrayal by a ruling class that has failed its people," Roy claimed that the nuclear explosions (and the consequent nationalist euphoria) had destroyed an important aspect of India's freedom: its capacity to articulate a different, noncolonial vision of the global order (9). She argued that the Indian government's decision should be read not as the defiance of a colonial West but as its own capitulation to the "ultimate coloniser." Nuclear weapons, she asserted passionately, "bury themselves like meat hooks deep in the base of our brains. They are purveyors of madness. They are the ultimate coloniser. Whiter than any white man that ever lived. The very heart of whiteness" (6). Dismissing the official claims that the tests were a response to "Western hypocrisy," Roy pointed out that the historical record of "the West" testified more to an arrogance about its coercive power than to hypocrisy.

Exposing Western hypocrisy—how much more exposed can they be? Colonialism, apartheid, slavery, ethnic cleansing, germ warfare, chemical weapons—they virtually invented it all. They have plundered nations, snuffed out civilizations, exterminated entire populations. They stand on the world's stage stark naked but entirely unembarrassed, because they know that they have more money, more food and bigger bombs than anybody else. They know they can wipe us out in the course of an ordinary working day. Personally, I'd say it is more arrogance than hypocrisy. (10)

An India that wanted to be different had now shown itself to be the real hypocrite. It had "traded" a "moral position" for membership in a colonial order.

I offer this brief summary of Roy's critique of India's decision as a good example of an alternative imagination of the global that utilizes but also transcends the limits of the national. Two things are particularly striking about this critique. First, it was a relatively courageous intellectual stance in terms of the national opposition and ridicule it was bound to—and did—receive within India. Roy had achieved a significant amount of publicity and goodwill just the year before for her literary achievements. Her antinuclear position not only risked all that but also invited charges of political naïveté on the part of a literary figure. Second, and most important, the criticism is distinctive because it produces an imagination of the global from within a national base but without allowing the national to colonize our understanding of the global. In other words, Roy's understanding of the global emerges from the national yet does not become subservient to it. The national community does not become the ethical boundary of the imagination or of political practice. Politics does not, should not, stop at the water's edge.

Roy begins by criticizing the decision on nationalist grounds. The Indian state has failed to deliver on its claims to the Indian nation and to the world. These claims are not based on national security, national power, or some form of national interest. The Indian state had failed to live up to its moral responsibility to itself and to humanity. In this critique, moral responsibility was not something that was to be left to other nations to deliver, contingent on the capacity of other nations or other people to live up to their responsibilities, or a social contract that one state had with others. It was a demand that the national Self made on itself, a commitment to the nation's own idea of what it was or wanted to be. It is on this level that Roy critiques the Indian state. When the national Self fails to live up to this responsibility, Roy threatens secession as one possible, justifiable response:

> If protesting against having a nuclear bomb implanted in my brain is anti-Hindu and anti-national, then I secede. I hereby declare myself an independent, mobile republic. I am a citizen of the earth. I own no territory. I have no flag. I'm female, but have nothing against eunuchs.[4] My policies are simple. I'm willing to sign any nuclear non-proliferation treaty or nuclear test ban treaty that's going. Immigrants are welcome. You can help me design our flag. (9)

Roy's threat to secede is important not as a practically possible act, I would argue, but as an imaginative claim that forces us to think beyond the moral community of the nation to other valuable forms of political association, possibly to an alternative understanding of the global. Roy draws on the existence of a powerful imagination of the national community to demand more responsible political practices from the state—practices that address the concerns not just of her own national community but also those of other human beings in the world. The national state is thus held responsible not only to those that it sees as its own people, but also to those that it might implicitly produce as Others. The possibility that the states representing these Others might be bankrupt in their moral responsibilities to their own people or to others is not enough, in Roy's critique, to disown one's own moral responsibility to all of humanity.

While Roy draws on the existence of a historically powerful imagination of the national Self, she does not reify it either. Her argument does not privilege her national community as the ultimate boundary of her politics. Such an argument would easily substitute a moral arrogance about one's nation for the military arrogance of others, privilege one nation, one configuration of the political Self, as the ultimate repository of both good and evil, and end up as a colonial moment. But Roy avoids that relapse by her willingness to question the historically received notion of an authentic India (15).

By problematizing the notion of any fixed or "authentic India," Roy brings home to us the potential limits of any essentialized national communities as empowerers of critical political action. She opens up the imagination to the possibility that the limits of our national boundaries need not be the limits of our political practices or our humanity. Other forms of political association are possible, desirable, and worth striving for. Secession is OK, maybe even desirable if it empowers us to act morally. Treason to one's inherited political community is not the ultimate crime. Failure to deliver on one's moral responsibility to other human beings is. There are therefore other possibilities, "other worlds," "other kinds of dreams," where "failure" is "feasible" and "honourable." And the world, as Roy points out, has "plenty of warriors . . . who go to war each day, knowing in advance that they will fail" (7).

In Roy's critique we can see both the empowering and the limiting aspects of historically inherited national imaginations as they seek to rearticulate the dominant constitutions of the global. Different productions of the global can therefore be read as invitations to constantly confront and renegotiate the historically given limits of the local and the national. Creative political agency lies not in reproducing the national, but in working in and through our historically given spaces of the local and the national to produce alternative forms of global solidarities.

Such reworkings can take place at many sites and in multiple ways.[5] What is interesting about such reworkings is not just how or where they take place but what existing privileges of the national Self they call into question. Proponents or critics of the global that do not offer a space for dissensus and difference, that do not encourage a self-reflexivity that engages and seeks to learn from various Others, can be seen as deeply complicit in the production of colonial globalities.

Notes

INTRODUCTION

1. Telugu is the official language of the region and is spoken by approximately 73 million people. *Desam* translates from Telugu as "country."

2. "Kingmaker and Technocrat," special report, *Business India*, May 4–17, 1998, 82–83.

3. Ibid.

4. He became chief minister after successfully splitting the Telugu Desam from the control of his father-in-law, N. T. Rama Rao. From 1995 to 1997 Naidu was instrumental in holding together an anticommunal coalition of left-of-center parties committed to preventing the Hindu right from coming to power at the national level. When the political equations changed after midterm elections, he broke rank to help the Hindu right sustain itself in power at the national level. There can be good reasons then to see his managerial approach as one more exercise in retaining power through the cultivation of a specific image.

5. See http://www.andhrapradesh.com/cm/weforum/sld034.htm.

6. Ibid.

7. See http://microsoft.com/corpinfo/press/1998/mar98/indiapr.htm.

8. "Kingmaker and Technocrat," 82.

9. See http://www.andhrapradesh.com/cm/weforum/sld037.htm.

10. See http://www.andhrapradesh.com/it/mait/sld045.htm.

11. "Bravo, Naidu!" editorial in the *Economic Times* 37, no. 122 (September 27, 1997); excerpted at http://www.andhrapradesh.com/cm/27sep.htm.

12. In his frequent presentations on the "window of opportunity" facing Andhra Pradesh, Naidu would note that there were "400,000 positions in the Information Technology industry [that were] internationally vacant." Of these, he would point out, "190,000 job vacancies [were] in the U.S. alone," http://www.andhrapradesh.com/cm/weforum/sld060.htm (accessed June 1998).

13. See, for instance, the National Informatics Policy Submission Paper presented by Naidu's government to the Indian central government, at http://www.andhrapradesh.com/National%20Informatics%20Policy.html.

14. Moreover India, unlike the United States, is highly centrist in practice. State governments are always under the threat of dismissal from the center, especially when they are ruled by different political parties. So the scope for independent action at the local level is exceedingly limited.

15. Lizette Alvarez, "Senate Votes to Increase Number of Foreigners Allowed in U.S. to Fill Technology Jobs," *New York Times,* May 19, 1998, C7.

16. See http://www.senate.gov/~abraham/Press/amercompet.html.

17. "H1 Visa Quota Hike by U.S. Greeted with Joy by IT Pros," *Deccan Chronicle,* May 22, 1998.

18. "The White House at Work," United Nations address, September 22, 1997, http://www.whitehouse.gov/WH/Work/092297.html.

19. "President's Remarks at the United Nations General Assembly," September 12, 2002, http://www.whitehouse.gov/news/releases/2002/09/20020912-1.html.

20. *The National Security Strategy of the United States of America,* 2002, http://www.whitehouse.gov/nsc/nss.html.

1. COLONIAL GLOBALITIES

1. The metaphor of home and abroad is a powerful and evocative image. Feminists and postcolonial theorists have used it before to problematize some easy assumptions of location and displacement. See Radhakrishnan (1996). Ruggie's notion of "multiperspectival" forms shares some similarities with postcolonial and feminist elaborations of the complexity of social identities. These connections, however, are not fully developed within Ruggie's arguments. See also Biddy Martin and Chandra Talpade Mohanty in de Lauretis (1986) and Adams (1989).

2. Wendt systematizes much of his earlier work in his *Social Theory of International Politics* (1999). I do not, however, deal with that more comprehensive framework here.

3. I do not mean to argue that this is particular only to historical materialism but that historical materialism has not been completely successful in shaking this legacy of orientalism.

4. Robert Cox (1986, 1987, 1991), among other neo-Gramscians, has explicitly dealt with the substantive issue of the global economy and the ways in which state understandings and policies have converged toward a focus on international competitiveness within this global economy. Other theorists in this tradition have extended Cox's pioneering work in specific directions (Gill 1993; Rupert 1995, 2000; Overbeek 1993). Rupert's analysis of the production of U.S. hegemony is exemplary in this regard.

5. These forces operate at the levels of the organization of production as social forces, of state/society complexes as forms of state, and of particular world orders. See Cox in Keohane (1986).

6. My analysis in this section draws on the work of the postcolonial historian Gyan Prakash. See the debate between Prakash (1990) and O'Hanlon and Washbrook (1992).

7. Mark Rupert's work, for instance, provides an extremely perceptive account of the ideology of globalization at the level of the U.S. national space. Locating the universality of globalization's claims in the context of the sectarian interests and resources behind that outcome, Rupert provides a powerful account of the battles that took place in the United States in the context of NAFTA and the WTO. His work is also unusual in explicitly recognizing the importance of the consensual aspect (following Hall) in the production of the "ideologies of globalization." But, as I show in the chapter on the United States, Rupert does not quite deliver on the politics of the interpretive and imaginative struggles that were carried on within this space.

8. James Meek, "One Boy's War . . . Bathed in Blood of His Family," *Observer*, April 6, 2003.

2. CRITICAL CONSTRUCTIVISM

1. I do not doubt that coercive power has an interpretive dimension while interpretive power has a materiality (that could be seen as coercive) to it. But I am somewhat wary of completely collapsing the distinction between the two.

2. The relational aspect is not affected by the fact that the someone in question may be the same person imagined or posited in a different spatio-temporal setting. Examples such as "I owe this to myself" or "I understand myself differently now" or "I demand this from myself" do not, in my opinion, make any difference to the relations being expressed between "I" and "myself." What is important is that the demand, obligation, or self-understanding already contains a relationship.

3. John McCain, "A Fight for Freedom," *Washington Post,* March 23, 2003, B07.

4. I adapt this from Sayer (1992).

3. GLOBALIZATION IN INDIA

1. For works broadly supportive of economic reform, see Bhagwati (1993), Cassen and Joshi (1995), Chelliah (1996), Jalan (1991, 1992), Lal (1988), and Srinivasan (1994). For a critical perspective on economic reforms, see Bhaduri and Nayyar (1996), Nayyar (1996), Kurien (1994, 1996), and Patnaik (1995). For broad overviews of Indian economic policy, see Bardhan (1984), Bhagwati and Desai (1970), Byres (1995), Chakravarty (1987), and Vaidyanathan (1995). For a more focused but critical debate on Indian industrial development (or the lack of it), see Ahluwalia (1985) and Nayyar (1994).

2. This happened when some sections in the media interpreted the presence of American phrases and spellings in the traditional budget document as evidence that Manmohan Singh had essentially drafted the budget on lines dictated by the IMF. Rao eventually prevailed on Singh to withdraw his resignation.

3. V. S. Sambandan, "What the Major Parties Promise," *Hindu Business Review,* April 24, 1996, 21.

4. "Indians Must Boycott MNC Goods: Patkar," *Hindu,* February 8, 1997, 5.

5. Ibid.

6. Javed Sayed, "Tarun Das Breathes Fire on MNC Entrants' One-Night Stand," *Economic Times,* March 20, 1996, 1; Sanjay Anand and Kingshuk Nag, "Balancing between 'Swadeshi' and Multinationals," *Sunday Times of India,* March 24, 1996, 16; "FICCI, ASSOCHAM Disagree over the Role of MNCs," *Times of India,* March 27, 1996, 1; Alok Mukherjee, "Home Ground but Still . . . ," *Hindu,* March 31, 1996, 13; CRR, "Indian Industry's Complaints about MNCs," *Hindu,* March 28, 1996, 14; Kingshuk Nag, "Industry Returns to 'Swadeshi' on Election Eve: Bid to Keep MNCs Away," *Times of India,* March 23, 1996, 1.

7. Medha Patkar, "Beyond the 'Outer Society,'" interview by Kamal Lodaya, *Economic Times,* January 28, 1996.

8. Rahul Bajaj, "Yes, I Believe Capital Does Have Colour," interview by N. Chandera Mohan, *Times of India,* January 9, 1998.

9. Peter Fuhrman with Michael Schuman, "Now We Are Our Own Masters," *Forbes,* May 23, 1994, 128–38.

10. Romesh Chunder Dutt, Dadabhai Naoroji, and Mahadev Govind

Ranade were some of the prominent economists in the earlier phase of the nationalist movement. In order to illustrate my broader point, I have chosen to rely on excerpts from Dutt's two-volume *The Economic History of India* (1901, 1903). Dutt was one of the first Indians to get into the Indian Civil Service—a colonial institution that was seen as the "steel frame" of the British Empire in India. Dutt retired voluntarily after twenty-six years of administrative service to actively participate in public life. In the course of such activities, he presided over the Indian National Congress in 1899, taught history at University College, London, and continuously engaged the British administration through his articles, writings, and letters. His economic writings were an important aspect of his political work and proved very significant in fueling the nationalist movement in subsequent years. D. R. Gadgil, a prominent Indian economist, points out in his 1959 introduction to Dutt's two-volume history—a history reprinted by the government of postcolonial India—that "Dutt's was almost the first history of a colonial regime written from the point of view of the subject of a colonial empire. It contains, in essence, a preview of what came later to be called the economics of colonialism." These ideas were so influential a part of the nationalist "commonsense" that much the same argument could be made by using the writings of others such as Naoroji (1901) or Ranade (Dasgupta 1993). For a more detailed and well-documented analysis of the writings and influence of these economists as well as a commentary on their contributions to the nationalist struggle, see Bipan Chandra (1966) and Dasgupta (1993).

11. There is an extensive debate among Indian economic historians on the nature, extent, and importance of the "drain theory" as well as the larger validity of the arguments of nationalist economic historians. Broadly divided into the Cambridge, Aligarh–JNU Marxist, and subaltern perspectives, these three schools of thought differ significantly on the interpretation they bring to these issues. One general axis of contention in recent years has been the interpretation of Indian history offered by the *Cambridge Economic History of India*, vol. 2. Another axis of contention concerns the criticism of Marxist historiography as nationalist and elitist by subaltern historians who, following Gramsci and poststructural theory, argue for a greater focus on the less legalistic and more spontaneous uprisings of the subaltern groups in the struggle against colonialism. On the subaltern perspective, see, in addition to the Subaltern Series, Guha (1997).

12. Cited in Seth (1995, 207); emphasis removed. Symbolic concessions to Gandhi apart, it was the Nehruvian approach that prevailed in the end.

13. It is true that as the nationalist movement progressed, it exhibited substantial differences from its earlier, more moderate phases. In its later stages, the nationalists did demand total independence from the British.

Significant sections within it also advocated and relied on a more forcible and violent struggle against the British. Mohandas Gandhi was important and influential but an outsider to the dominant modernizing strand within the nationalist movement. He was important in deepening the social basis of the nationalist movement to incorporate India's rural masses through a more traditional political rhetoric. Notwithstanding Gandhi and other traditionally powerful strands of imagining India within the nationalist social imaginary, the leading understandings of an independent India remained focused on separating it from the control of the British state but not from the achievements of Western modernity. See Chatterjee (1986).

14. See Finance Minister Shanmukham Chetty's speech (Ministry of Finance 1990, 1).

15. See Nehru's statement in the Constituent Assembly (Legislative), New Delhi, March 5, 1948 (excerpted in Nehru 1949, 72).

16. This involved, at one level, the negotiated distribution and rearrangement of millions of people, resources, territory, financial/industrial assets, and liabilities.

17. See Nehru's speech in the House of the People, New Delhi, December 15, 1952 (excerpted in Nehru 1954, 87).

18. Nehru in a speech in the House of the People, New Delhi, December 15, 1952 (excerpted in Nehru 1954, 83).

19. Important differences existed between the Soviet and Indian approaches to planning, though the Mahalanobis model underlying the Second Five Year Plan in India shared certain common themes with Soviet models of planning in laying stress on heavy industries.

20. Exports were periodically emphasized as a way of earning the necessary foreign exchange, but this stress was never predominant. It also conflicted with the stronger desire to change the colonially inherited economic structure. In the end, it was always the transformation of the inherited economic structure that took precedence.

21. See Shanmukham Chetty's presentation of the government's budget in India (Ministry of Finance 1990, 11, 16).

22. See, for example, Indira Gandhi's *Person to Person* broadcast over All India Radio, August 7, 1966 (excerpted in Gandhi 1971, 106).

23. Mukherjee 1996. A careful review of the various materials gathered in the course of my field research supports my decision to see this as a key policy document. It brings together quite competently many of the arguments of the economic reformers and presents a careful and comprehensive map of the emerging worldview of the Indian government after the end of the Cold War and nearly five years after economic reforms. As a document that not only articulates Indian economic policy but also situates it in relation to Indian foreign policy, this is doubly valuable. Moreover, Mukherjee

delivered this speech to the members of the Indian diplomatic service when he was the minister of external affairs, which allows a reading of this document as expressive of the dominant understandings of a government committed to economic reforms.

24. He assumes a straightforward link between a targeted growth rate, the specific level of investment needed to finance that growth rate, and the associated incremental capital-output ratio in the economy.

25. The growth rate was 3.5 percent per annum from 1960 to 1980—a growth rate made famous (or infamous) as the "Hindu rate of growth" by Indian economists. There is an enormous literature on the causes of this stagnation. See Ahluwalia (1985) and Nayyar (1994) for good overviews of the debate on this subject.

26. On the economic crisis of 1991 see Jalan (1993).

27. In the conditions of domestic savings prevailing then, i.e., without an additional internal mobilization of economic resources.

28. This fear has been articulated quite explicitly by government officials in various seminars and presentations.

29. Such claims are matched by those of other official spokespersons who argued that a failure to recognize the strength of the new national Self stems either out of some form of ignorance (about economic realities, the global economy, changed conditions) or some sort of psychological lack (inferiority complex, fear of the East India Company, fear of competition).

30. Both represented a throwing out—an externalization—of the foreign Other.

4. GLOBALIZATION IN THE UNITED STATES

1. See U.S. Senate Hearings (1993), *National Economic Strategies for a Global Economy* and *Strengthening America to Compete in the Global Economy.*

2. See Michael L. Wheeler, "Global Diversity: Reality, Opportunity, and Challenge," special advertising section, *Business Week*, December 1, 1997, beginning on p. 75.

3. See the remarks of John Sweeney, president of the AFL-CIO, at Economic Strategy Institute Conference, April 16, 1997, http://www.aflcio.org/publ/speech97/sp0416.htm.

4. At the other end of the spectrum from such organizations lies the "Statement of Principles" of the Project for the New American Century. Consisting of actors who are extremely powerful in the second Bush administration, such as Dick Cheney, Donald Rumsfeld, and Paul Wolfowitz, the explicitly articulated claims of this group offer a "strategic vision

of America's role in the world" structured around "rally[ing] support" and accepting "the responsibilities of global leadership." See http://www .newamericancentury.org/statementofprinciples.htm.

5. See the statement of Alan A. Reich, the president of the National Organization on Disability, who notes, "Since the U.S. is a leader, one can assert with pride that the U.S. has provided leadership in the world in the area of disability." In beginning with the proposition that the U.S. is a leader, Mr. Reich comes close to naturalizing that trait as the nation's very state of being. Quote from Wheeler, "Global Diversity," n.p.

6. I would acknowledge that there is a particular discourse of leadership that is based on meeting the needs of the Other, one that portrays the United States as aiding the poor, the hungry, the exploited, the oppressed, or otherwise unfortunate countries and peoples of the world. This is the discourse that empowers both foreign aid and humanitarian intervention (in places such as Somalia and, more recently, in Iraq). However, in nearly all these cases, the voices of these Others do not enter the picture at all. The United States determines what the needs of the Others are and responds as it deems fit. The response might be humanitarian and based on an assessment of the Others' needs, but that assessment is not one in which the latter's voices are represented in the determination of these needs or one that is dialogical. I thank Bud Duvall for alerting me to this thread in American self-conception.

7. Mallaby 2002; Robert Cooper, "The New Liberal Imperialism," Observer, April 7, 2002, http://www.observer.co.uk/Print/0,3858,4388912 ,00.html.

8. Mallaby is an editorial writer for the Washington Post.

9. I am, quite arguably in this specific instance, reading Blair as one of the more effective articulators of the American imagination of the world. Blair, speech to the British Labour Party Conference, October 2, 2001, http: //politics.guardian.co.uk/labourconference2001/story/0,1220,561988,00 .html.

10. Report released by the White House, December 1999, http://usinfo .state.gov/regional/ar/natsec2k.htm.

5. PRODUCTIONS OF THE GLOBAL

1. Charles Babington, Washington Post, March 11, 1999.

2. Fergal Keene, BBC News, April 7, 2003.

3. Isabel Hilton, "Getting Away with Murder," Guardian, November 21, 2000.

4. Interview with Bill Moyers, *NOW*, September 20, 2002, PBS transcript.

5. Karen Brandon, "Should Troops Be U.S. Citizens?" *Chicago Tribune,* online edition, April 13, 2003; Valerie Alvord, "Non-citizens Fight and Die for Adopted Country," *USA Today,* April 8, 2003. One report observes, "Around half of new recruits to the armed forces in some LA areas are non-citizens whose service in the military will accelerate their route to citizenship." See Duncan Campbell, "Dying to Belong," *Guardian,* April 22, 2003.

6. William Booth, "Sweat of Their Brows Reshapes Economy," *Washington Post,* July 13, 1998, A01, http://www.washingtonpost.com/wp-srv /longterm/meltingpot/melt4.htm.

7. This fits in with the general profile of immigrant labor in the United States where, as Booth points out, "Immigrants today do some of the dirtiest, most difficult and dangerous work in America, the work that native-born Americans—of any ethnicity or race—often will no longer do, or no longer do for the wages offered" (ibid.).

8. According to one report, Andhra Pradesh's per capita income is 75 percent of the national average, its literacy levels are below those of the national level, and it has "the highest incidence of child labor in India." See R. J. Rajendra Prasad, "Making His Dream Come True," *Hindu,* July 19, 1998, 12.

9. See http://www.stph.net/scheme/ehtpscheme/ehtpscheme.html.

10. See "STPH Exports Up 100% at Rs. 274 Crores [$69.37 million]," http://www.stph.net/clippings/stphexports.html.

11. See "Hyderabad Seems to Be the Choice for ERP Training," http: //www.stph.net/clippings/erparticle.html.

12. *Deccan Chronicle,* May 15, 1998; reproduced at http://www .andhrapradesh.com/cm/into%20the%20millenium1508.html.

13. See http://www.senate.gov/~feinstein/speeches/h1b.html.

14. See http://www3.senate.gov/search/s97_cgi.ex...navigate'off&view Template'defauiep%2Esn2.

15. See http://www.senate.gov/~ashcroft/compete.htm.

16. See http://www3.senate.gov/search/s97_cgi.ex...navigate'off&view Template'defauiep%2Esn2.

17. Ibid.

18. See http://www.senate.gov/~rpc/rva/1052/052138.htm.

19. See http://www.andhrapradesh.com/cm/CMSPEECH.html.

20. See http://www.andhrapradesh.com/National%20Informatics%20 Policy.html.

21. The White House, Office of the Press Secretary, remarks by the

president at the U.S. Coast Guard Academy's 119th commencement, Cadet Memorial Field, U.S. Coast Guard Academy, New London, Connecticut, May 17, 2000, http://www.pub.whitehouse.gov/uri-res/I2R?urn:pdi://oma.eop.gov.us/2000/5/17/4.text.1.

22. Art Borjal, "The Filipino Can!" *Philippine Star,* May 11, 2000, http://www.philstar.com/datedata/g11-may11/edi2.htm.

23. Seth Mydans, "National Pride over a Virus in Philippines," *New York Times,* May 12, 2000, C1.

24. See Varadarajan (1998) for a good critique of such explanations.

25. Comprehensive Test Ban Treaty Fact Sheet, White House, September 10, 1996, http://www.acda.gov/factshee/wmd/nuclear/ctbt/ctbtfs.htm.

26. "UN Adopts Comprehensive Test Ban Treaty," press statement by Secretary of State Warren Christopher, Department of State, Washington, D.C., September 11, 1996, http://www.state.gov/www/global/arms/960911.html.

27. Statement to the UN First Committee General Debate by John D. Holum, U.S. Arms Control and Disarmament Agency, October 14, 1998, http://www.acda.gov/speeches/holum/unfc.htm.

28. "Article-by-Article Analysis of the Comprehensive Nuclear Test Ban Treaty," http://www.acda.gov/ctbtpage/preamble.htm.

29. Events and Campaigns: Nuclear Testing," http://www.peacenet.org/disarm/testing.html.

30. Fareed Zakaria, "Facing Up to Nuclear Reality," *Newsweek,* June 8, 1998.

31. Jaswant Singh, "Against Nuclear Apartheid," *Foreign Affairs,* September/October 1998, 41–52.

32. Francois Gire, "New Delhi Wished to Create the Irreversible," *Le Monde,* May 22, 1998, http://www.meadev.nic.in/govt/monde.htm.

CONCLUSION

1. The signers identified themselves as "part of a coalition of more than 60 non-profit organizations that favor democratic, localized, ecologically sound alternatives to current practices and policies." Some of the NGOs listed were Global Exchange, Institute for Agriculture and Trade Policy, Friends of the Earth, Rainforest Action Network, Earth Island Institute, International Forum on Globalization, Sierra Club, Greenpeace U.S., 50 Years Is Enough: U.S. Network for Global Economic Justice, People-Centered Development Forum, the Council of Canadians, and the Institute for Policy Studies—Global Economy Project.

2. See http://www.turnpoint.org for these advertisements.

3. "Global Monoculture," *New York Times,* November 15, 1999, A6–7.

4. This is a reference to the Shiv Sena's (a far-right Indian political party) claim—described early on in Roy's essay—that the nuclear tests proved that "we [Indians] are not eunuchs anymore."

5. In the context of September 11, see, for instance, the aims of the advocacy organization September Eleventh Families for Peaceful Tomorrows, http://www.peacefultomorrows.org/mission.html.

Works Cited

Adams, Mary Louise. 1989. "There's No Place Like Home: On the Place of Identity in Feminist Politics." *Feminist Review* 31: 22–33.

Agarwal, Shriman Narayan. 1944. *The Gandhian Plan of Economic Development for India.* Bombay: Padma.

Ahluwalia, Isher Judge. 1985. *Industrial Growth in India: Stagnation since the Mid-Sixties.* Delhi: Oxford University Press.

Ahluwalia, Isher Judge, and I. M. D. Little, eds. 1998. *India's Economic Reforms and Development: Essays for Manmohan Singh.* New Delhi: Oxford University Press.

Althusser, Louis. 1971. *Lenin and Philosophy and Other Essays.* Trans. Ben Brewster. New York: Monthly Review Press.

Anderson, Benedict R. O'G. 1991. *Imagined Communities.* London: Verso.

Appadurai, Arjun. 1996. *Modernity at Large.* Minneapolis: University of Minnesota Press.

Bardhan, Pranab. 1984. *The Political Economy of Development in India.* Oxford, UK: Blackwell.

Bhabha, Homi. 1994. *The Location of Culture.* London: Routledge.

Bhaduri, Amit, and Deepak Nayyar. 1996. *The Intelligent Person's Guide to Liberalization.* New Delhi: Penguin Books.

Bhagwati, Jagdish. 1993. *India in Transition: Freeing the Economy.* Oxford: Clarendon Press.

———. 1998. "The Design of Indian Development." In *India's Economic Reforms and Development: Essays for Manmohan Singh,* ed. Isher J. Ahluwalia and I. M. D. Little, 23–39. New Delhi: Oxford University Press.

Bhagwati, Jagdish, and Padma Desai. 1970. *India: Planning for Industrialization: Industrialization and Trade Policies since 1951.* London: Oxford University Press.

Bose, P. K., and M. Mukherjee, eds. 1985. *P. C. Mahalanobis: Papers on Planning.* Calcutta: Statistical Pub. Society.

Burtless, Gary, et al. 1998. *Globaphobia: Confronting Fears about Open Trade.* Washington, D.C.: Brookings Institution.

Byres, Terence J., ed. 1995. *The State and Development Planning in India.* Delhi: Oxford University Press.

Campbell, David. 1992. *Writing Security: United States Foreign Policy and the Politics of Identity.* Minneapolis: University of Minnesota Press.

———. 1993. *Politics without Principle.* Boulder, CO: Lynne Rienner.

Cassen, Robert, and Vijay Joshi, eds. 1995. *India: The Future of Economic Reform.* Delhi: Oxford University Press.

Castoriadis, Cornelius. 1987. *The Imaginary Institution of Society.* Trans. Kathleen Blamey. Cambridge: MIT Press.

Chakrabarty, Dipesh. 2001. *Provincializing Europe.* Princeton, NJ: Princeton University Press.

Chakravarty, Sukhamoy. 1987. *Development Planning: The Indian Experience.* Oxford, UK: Clarendon Press.

Chandra, Bipan. 1966. *The Rise and Growth of Economic Nationalism in India: Economic Policies of Indian National Leadership, 1880–1905.* New Delhi: People's Publishing House.

Chatterjee, Partha. 1986. *Nationalist Thought and the Colonial World: A Derivative Discourse?* London: Zed Press.

———, ed. 1992. *Subaltern Studies.* Vol. 7. New Delhi: Oxford University Press.

———. 1993. *The Nation and Its Fragments: Colonial and Postcolonial Histories.* Princeton, NJ: Princeton University Press.

———, ed. 1998. *Wages of Freedom.* New Delhi: Oxford University Press.

Chelliah, Raja J. 1996. *Towards Sustainable Growth: Essays in Fiscal and Financial Sector Reforms.* Delhi: Oxford University Press.

Cox, R. W. 1986. "Social Forces, States, and World Orders." In *Neorealism and Its Critics,* ed. Robert Keohane. New York: Columbia University Press.

———. 1987. *Production, Power, and World Order: Social Forces in the Making of History.* New York: Columbia University Press.

———. 1991. "The Global Political Economy and Social Choice." In *The New Era of Global Competition: State Policy and Market Power,* ed. Daniel Drache and Meric S. Gertler. Montreal: McGill/Queen's University Press.

Czempiel, Ernst-Otto, and James Rosenau, eds. 1989. *Global Changes and Theoretical Challenges.* Lexington, MA: Lexington Books.

Dasgupta, Ajit K. 1993. *A History of Indian Economic Thought.* London: Routledge.

Davis, Mike. 2001. *Late Victorian Holocausts.* New York: Verso.

de Lauretis, Teresa, ed. 1986. *Feminist Studies/Critical Studies.* Bloomington: Indiana University Press.

Djebar, Assia. 1993. *Fantasia: An Algerian Cavalcade.* Portsmouth: Heineman.

Doty, Roxanne Lynn. 1996. *Imperial Encounters: The Politics of Representation in North-South Relations.* Minneapolis: University of Minnesota Press.

Dutt, Romesh Chunder. 1901. *The Economic History of India.* Vol. 1. New Delhi: Publications Division, Ministry of Information and Broadcasting, Government of India.

———. 1903. *The Economic History of India.* Vol. 2. New Delhi: Publications Division, Ministry of Information and Broadcasting, Government of India.

Gaddis, John Lewis. 2002. "A Grand Strategy of Transformation." *Foreign Policy,* no. 133 (November/December): 50–57.

Gandhi, Indira. 1971. *Selected Speeches of Indira Gandhi, January 1966–1969.* New Delhi: Publications Division, Ministry of Information and Broadcasting, Government of India.

Garten, Jeffrey E. 1997. *The Big Ten: The Big Emerging Markets and How They Will Change Our Lives.* New York: Basic Books.

Ghose, Arundhati. 1997. "Negotiating the CTBT: India's Security Concerns and Nuclear Disarmament." *Journal of International Affairs* 51, no. 1: 239–61.

Gill, Stephen, ed. 1993. *Gramsci, Historical Materialism, and International Relations.* Cambridge: Cambridge University Press.

Gill, Stephen R., and D. Law. 1988. *The Global Political Economy: Perspectives, Problems, and Policies.* Baltimore: The Johns Hopkins University Press.

Guha, Ranajit, ed. 1997. *A Subaltern Studies Reader, 1986–1995.* Minneapolis: University of Minnesota Press.

Habib, Irfan. 1988. *Interpreting Indian History.* Shillong: North-Eastern Hill University Publications.

Hall, Stuart. 1985. "Signification, Representation, Ideology: Althusser and the Post-Structuralist Debates. *Critical Studies in Mass Communication* 2, no. 2: 91–114.

———. 1988. "The Toad in the Garden: Thatcherism among the Theorists." In *Marxism and the Interpretation of Culture,* ed. Cary Nelson and Lawrence Grossberg. Urbana: University of Illinois Press.

Hartz, Louis. 1955. *The Liberal Tradition in America: An Interpretation of American Political Thought since the Revolution*. New York: Harcourt, Brace.

Hochschild, Adam. 1998. *King Leopold's Ghost*. New York: Mariner Books.

Hunt, Michael H. 1987. *Ideology and U.S. Foreign Policy*. New Haven, CT: Yale University Press.

Ikenberry, John. 2002. "America's Imperial Ambition." *Foreign Affairs* 81, no. 5: 44–60.

Inayatullah, Naeem, and David Blaney. 2001. "International Relations and the Problem of Difference." Book manuscript.

Jaffrelot, Christophe. 1996. *The Hindu Nationalist Movement in India*. New York: Columbia University Press.

Jalan, Bimal, ed. 1992. *The Indian Economy: Problems and Prospects*. New Delhi: Viking.

———. 1993. *India's Economic Crisis: The Way Ahead*. Delhi: Oxford University Press.

Keohane, Robert O., ed. 1986. *Neorealism and Its Critics*. New York: Columbia University Press.

———. 2000. "Governance in a Partially Globalized World." Presidential address, American Political Science Association. Published in *American Political Science Review* 95, no. 1 (March 2001): 1–13.

Kolko, Joyce. 1988. *Restructuring the Global Economy*. New York: Pantheon Books.

Krishna, Sankaran. 1999. *Postcolonial Insecurities*. Minneapolis: University of Minnesota Press.

———. 2001. "You Talkin' to Me? Race, Amnesia, and the Education of International Relations." Paper presented at the annual meeting of the International Studies Association, March 21–26, Chicago.

Krugman, Paul. 1994. "Competitiveness: A Dangerous Obsession." *Foreign Affairs* 73: 28–44.

Kumar, Dharma, ed. 1983. *The Cambridge Economic History of India*. Vol. 2. C. *1757–1970*. Cambridge: Cambridge University Press.

Kurien, C. T. 1994. *Global Capitalism and the Indian Economy*. Hyderabad: Orient Longman Ltd.

———. 1996. *Economic Reforms and the People*. Delhi: Madhyam Books.

Laclau, Ernesto. 1977. *Politics and Ideology in Marxist Theory*. London: Verso.

Lal, Deepak. 1988. *Cultural Stability and Economic Stagnation: India, c. 1500 BC–AD 1980*. Oxford: Clarendon Press.

Landry, Donna, and Gerald Maclean, eds. 1996. *The Spivak Reader*. London: Routledge.

Legro, Jeffrey W. 1996. "Culture and Preferences in the International Cooperation Two-Step." *American Political Science Review* 90, no. 1: 118–37.

Lemann, Nicholas. 2002. "The Next World Order." *New Yorker,* April 1.

Lindqvist, Sven. 1996. *"Exterminate All the Brutes."* New York: New Press.

Lipset, Seymour Martin. 1963. *The First New Nation: The United States in Historical and Comparative Perspective.* New York: Basic Books.

Löwy, M. (1981). *The Politics of Combined and Uneven Development.* London: Verso.

Macpherson, C. B. 1962. *The Political Theory of Possessive Individualism: Hobbes to Locke.* Oxford: Oxford University Press.

Mallaby, Sebastian. 2002. "The Reluctant Imperialist." *Foreign Affairs* 81, no. 2: 2–7.

Martin, Biddy, and Chandra Talpade Mohanty. 1986. "Feminist Politics: What's Home Got to Do with It?" In *Feminist Studies/Critical Studies,* ed. Teresa de Lauretis, 191–212. Bloomington: Indiana University Press.

Mehta, Uday Singh. 1999. *Liberalism and Empire.* Chicago: University of Chicago Press.

Ministry of Finance, Department of Economic Affairs. 1990. *Budget Speeches of Union Finance Ministers, 1947–48 to 1990–91.* New Delhi: Government of India.

Mukherjee, Pranab. 1996. "Economic Dimensions of India's Foreign Policy." Tenth Indira Gandhi Memorial Lecture, February 6. New Delhi: Association of Indian Diplomats.

Muppidi, Himadeep. 1999. "Postcoloniality and the Production of International Insecurity." In *Cultures of Insecurity: States, Communities, and the Production of Danger,* ed. Jutta Weldes et al. Minneapolis: University of Minnesota Press.

Naoroji, Dadabhai. 1901. *Poverty and Un-British Rule in India.* London: S. Sonnenschein.

Nayyar, Deepak, ed. 1994. *Industrial Growth and Stagnation: The Debate in India.* Bombay: Oxford University Press, for Sameeksha Trust.

———. 1996. *Economic Liberalization in India.* Calcutta: Center for Studies in Social Science.

Nehru, Jawaharlal. 1949. *Independence and After: A Collection of the More Important Speeches.* Delhi: Publications Division, Ministry of Information and Broadcasting, Government of India.

———. 1954. *Speeches, 1949–1953.* Delhi: Publications Division, Ministry of Information and Broadcasting, Government of India.

———. 1961. *India's Foreign Policy: Selected Speeches.* Delhi: Publications Division, Ministry of Information and Broadcasting, Government of India.

———. 1964. *Jawaharlal Nehru: Excerpts from His Writings and Speeches.* Delhi: Publications Division, Ministry of Information and Broadcasting, Government of India.

Nye, Joseph. 2001. "Globalization's Democratic Deficit." *Foreign Affairs* 80, no. 4: 2–6.

O'Hanlon, Rosalind, and David Washbrook. 1992. "After Orientalism: Culture, Criticism, and Politics in the Third World." *Comparative Studies in Society and History* 34, no. 1: 141–67.

Overbeek, H. W., ed. 1993. *Restructuring Hegemony in the Global Political Economy.* London: Routledge.

Overbeek, H. W., and Kees Van Der Pijl. 1993. "Restructuring Capital and Restructuring Hegemony: Neoliberalism and the Unmaking of the Postwar Order." In *Restructuring Hegemony in the Global Political Economy,* ed. H. W. Overbeek, 1–27. London: Routledge.

Patnaik, Prabhat. 1995. *Whatever Happened to Imperialism and Other Essays.* New Delhi: Tulika.

———. 1998. "Political Strategies of Economic Development." In *Wages of Freedom,* ed. Partha Chatterjee, 37–60. New Delhi: Oxford University Press.

Perot, H. Ross. 1993. *Not for Sale at Any Price: How We Can Save America for Our Children.* New York: Hyperion.

Planning Commission. 1952. *The First Five Year Plan: A Summary.* Delhi: Government of India.

———. 1956. *Second Five Year Plan: A Draft Outline.* New Delhi: Government of India.

Porter, Michael. 1990. *The Competitive Advantage of Nations.* New York: Free Press.

Prahalad, C. K., and Gary Hamel. 1994. *Competing for the Future.* Boston: Harvard Business School Press.

Prakash, G. 1990. "Writing Post-Orientalist Histories of the Third World: Perspectives from Indian Historiography." *Comparative Studies in Society and History* 32, no. 2: 383–408.

———. 1992. "Can the 'Subaltern' Ride? A Reply to O'Hanlon and Washbrook." *Comparative Studies in Society and History* 34, no. 1: 168–84.

Radhakrishnan, R. 1996. *Diasporic Mediations: Between Home and Location.* Minneapolis: University of Minnesota Press.

Rao, P. V. Narasimha. 1995. *P. V. Narasimha Rao, Selected Speeches.* Vols. 1–4. New Delhi: Publications Division, Ministry of Information and Broadcasting, Government of India.

Reich, Robert. 1991. *The Work of Nations.* New York: Knopf.

Roberts, Brad, ed. 1996. *New Forces in the World Economy.* Cambridge: MIT Press.

Roy, Arundhati. 1998. *The End of Imagination.* Special Publication, August 6. Chennai: Frontline/Kasturi.

Ruggie, J. G. 1982. "International Regimes, Transactions, and Change: Embedded Liberalism in the Postwar Economic Order." *International Organization* 36, no. 2: 379–415.

———. 1993. "Territoriality and Beyond: Problematizing Modernity in International Relations." *International Organization* 47, no. 1: 139–74.

———. 1994. "At Home Abroad, Abroad at Home: International Liberalisation and Domestic Stability in the New World Economy." *Millennium* 24, no. 3: 507–26.

Rupert, Mark. 1995. *Producing Hegemony.* Cambridge: Cambridge University Press.

———. 2000. *Ideologies of Globalization.* London: Routledge.

Sachs, Wolfgang, ed. 1992. *The Development Dictionary.* London: Zed.

Said, Edward. 1994. *Culture and Imperialism.* New York: Vintage.

Sayer, Andrew. 1992. *Method in Social Science: A Realist Approach.* London: Routledge.

Seth, Sanjay. 1995. *Marxist Theory and Nationalist Politics.* New Delhi: Sage.

Shapiro, Michael. 1992. *Reading the Postmodern Polity.* Minneapolis: University of Minnesota Press.

Singh, Tarlok. 1969. *Towards an Integrated Society: Reflections on Planning, Social Policy, and Rural Institutions.* Westport, CT: Greenwood.

Spivak, Gayatri. 1999. *A Critique of Postcolonial Reason.* Cambridge: Harvard University Press.

Spurr, David. 1993. *The Rhetoric of Empire.* Durham, NC: Duke University Press.

Srinivasan, T. N. 1994. "India's Economic Reforms: Tasks Ahead." Address at the seminar on Structural Adjustment and Policy Reforms: Perspectives from International Experiences, April 4. New Delhi: Indian Council for Research on International Economic Relations.

Thakurdas, Sir Purushotamdas, J. R. D. Tata, G. D. Birla, et al. 1944. *A Brief Memorandum Outlining a Plan of Economic Development for India.* New York: Penguin.

Tharoor, Shashi. 1997. *India: From Midnight to the Millennium.* New York: Arcade.

Thygesen, Niels, Yutaka Kosai, and Robert Z. Lawrence. 1996. *Globalization and Trilateral Labor Markets: Evidence and Implications.* New York: Trilateral Commission.

Todorov, Tzvetan. 1999. *The Conquest of America.* Norman: University of Oklahoma Press.

Tomlinson, John. 1991. *Cultural Imperialism*. Baltimore: The Johns Hopkins University Press.

U.S. Congress, Joint Economic Committee. 1992. *High Wage Jobs in a Competitive Global Economy*. Washington, DC.

U.S. Department of Commerce. 1994. *Competing to Win in a Global Economy*. Washington, DC.

U.S. Senate Hearings. 1993. *National Economic Strategies for a Global Economy*. Washington, DC.

———. 1993. *Strengthening America to Compete in the Global Economy*. Washington, DC.

———. 1994. *U.S. Competitiveness and Trade Policy in the Global Economy*. Washington, DC.

Vaidyanathan, A. 1995. *The Indian Economy: Crisis, Response, and Prospects*. New Delhi: Orient Longman.

Van Der Pijl, Kees. 1993. "The Sovereignty of Capital Impaired: Social Forces and Codes of Conduct for Multinational Corporations." In *Restructuring Hegemony in the Global Political Economy*, ed. H. W. Overbeek, 28–57. London: Routledge.

Varadarajan, Latha. 1998. "Making Sense of India's Nuclear Tests." Paper presented to Minnesota International Relations Colloquium, Department of Political Science, University of Minnesota.

Walt, Stephen. 2002. "American Primacy: Its Prospects and Pitfalls." *Naval War College Review* 55, no. 2: 9–29.

Waltz, Kenneth. 1999. "Globalization and Governance." James Madison Lecture. American Political Science Association, *Political Science Online,* www.apsanet.org.

Weldes, Jutta. 1999. *Constructing National Interests*. Minneapolis: University of Minnesota Press.

Weldes, Jutta, Mark Laffey, Hugh Gusterson, and Raymond Duvall, eds. 1999. *Cultures of Insecurity*. Minneapolis: University of Minnesota Press.

Wendt, Alexander E. 1987. "The Agent-Structure Problem in International Relations Theory." *International Organization* 41, no. 3: 335–70.

———. 1992. "Anarchy Is What States Make of It: The Social Construction of Power Politics." *International Organization* 46, no. 2: 391–425.

———. 1994. "Collective Identity Formation and the International State." *American Political Science Review* 88, no. 2: 384–96.

———. 1999. *Social Theory of International Politics*. Cambridge: Cambridge University Press.

Index

HIMADEEP MUPPIDI is assistant professor of political science at Vassar College.